THEMATIC UNIT

Sports

Written by Sherri McLeroy

W9-AEC-046

Teacher Created Materials, Inc.
6421 Industry Way
Westminster, CA 92683
www.teachercreated.com
©*1997 Teacher Created Materials, Inc.*
Reprinted, 2003
Made in U.S.A.
ISBN-1-55734-588-0

Illustrated by
Wendy Chang

Contributing Editor
Walter Kelly

Cover Art by
Sue Fullam

Table of Contents

Introduction

Sports is an exciting whole language unit about sports around the world, the Olympics, untold sports stories, and the importance of exercise and nutrition. The unit highlights three selections of children's literature—*Casey at the Bat* by Ernest Lawrence Thayer, *The Greatest Sports Stories Never Told* by Bruce Nash and Allan Zullo, and *The Winning Stroke* by Matt Christopher. Activities have been suggested to enhance all of these literature selections. The unit also highlights Matt Christopher as a sports author and gives some suggested author study ideas. In addition, theme-related activities in all curriculum areas are included. A wide variety of hands-on and literature-based activities with suggestions for cooperative learning are also included. Furthermore, a culminating activity has been suggested which would allow students to synthesize their knowledge about sports.

This thematic unit includes the following:

- ☐ **Literature Selections**—summaries of three children's books with related lessons that cross the curriculum

- ☐ **Poetry**—suggestions for guiding students to write and publish sports poetry

- ☐ **Author Study**—activities and suggestions for conducting author study on Matt Christopher

- ☐ **Writing Ideas**—writing activity suggestions for students to create and publish their own written works

- ☐ **Bulletin Board Ideas**—suggestions and plans for creating interactive bulletin boards

- ☐ **Homework**—meaningful homework suggestions

- ☐ **Curriculum Connections**—activities in language arts, math, science, social studies, art, music, physical education, and health

- ☐ **Group Projects**—suggested cooperative learning activities

- ☐ **Culminating Activity**—a conclusion to celebrate the sports theme and synthesize student learning to produce a product or engage in an activity that can be shared with others

- ☐ **Bibliography**—suggestions for additional fiction and nonfiction books on the theme

> **To keep this valuable resource intact so that it can be used year after year, you may wish to punch holes in the pages and store them in a three-ring binder.**

Introduction *(cont.)*

Why a Balanced Approach?

The strength of a balanced language approach is that it involves children in using all modes of communication—reading, writing, listening, illustrating, and doing. Communication skills are interconnected and integrated into lessons that emphasize the whole of language. Implicit to this approach is our knowledge that every whole—including individual words—is composed of parts, and directed study of those parts can help a student to master the whole. Experience and research tell us that regular attention to phonics, other word attack skills, spelling, etc., develops reading mastery, thereby completing the unity of the whole language experience. The child is thus led to read, write, spell, speak, and listen confidently in response to a literature experience introduced by the teacher. In these ways, language skills grow rapidly, stimulated by direct practice, involvement, and interest in the topic at hand.

Why Thematic Planning?

One very useful tool for implementing an integrated balanced language program is thematic planning. By choosing a theme with correlative literature selections for a unit of study, a teacher can plan activities throughout the day that lead to a cohesive, in-depth study of the topic. Students will be practicing and applying their skills in meaningful contexts. Consequently, they will tend to learn and retain more. Both teachers and students will be freed from a day that is broken into unrelated segments of isolated drill and practice.

Why Cooperative Learning?

Besides academic skills and content, students need to learn social skills. No longer can this area of development be taken for granted. Students must learn to work cooperatively in groups in order to function well in modern society. Group activities should be a regular part of school life, and teachers should consciously include social objectives as well as academic objectives in their planning. For example, a group working together to write a report may need to select a leader. The teacher should make clear to the students the qualities of good leader-follower group interactions just as he or she would state and monitor the academic goals of the project.

Why Big Books?

An excellent cooperative, balanced language activity is the production of Big Books. Groups of students or a whole class can apply their language skills, content knowledge, and creativity to produce Big Books that can become a part of the classroom library to be read and reread. These books make excellent culminating projects for sharing beyond the classroom with parents, librarians, other classes, etc. Big Books can be produced in many contexts, and this thematic unit book contains suggestions for at least one situation that you may find effective. Needless to say, both teachers and researchers have found this type of activity to be one of the most powerful methods of synthesizing knowledge, allowing students to internalize learning in a permanent form.

Casey at the Bat

by Ernest Lawrence Thayer

Summary

Casey at the Bat is a ballad of the republic that was sung in the year 1888. It is a wonderful story about a young boy named Casey who is an overconfident baseball player. He procrastinates about going to his baseball game because he is so sure he will not be late. When he finally arrives late to the game, the meanest umpire of the league gives him a not-too-cheerful greeting. His team members are not very pleased with him either.

The game begins, and Casey's team falls behind. The fans and the team desperately hope that Casey will get to bat because it is the end of the game and his team has two outs. Two players who are not very good batters precede Casey. The crowd is surprised and pleased when both players make great hits and get on base. Confidently, Casey steps up to bat as the crowd cheers him on. Tension builds when Casey lets two strikes go by without a care. The third pitch is thrown, and Casey swings with all his might. The crowd stands stunned while they watch Casey strike out.

In the end, he walks home with his dad, the umpire, and realizes that he should not "count his hits before they are pitched."

The outline below is a suggested plan for using the various activities and ideas that are presented in this unit. You should adapt these ideas to fit your own classroom situation.

Sample Plan

Lesson 1
- Chart predictions about the story. (page 6, Setting the Stage)
- Read the story for enjoyment. (page 6, Enjoying the Book)
- Complete the "Take Me Out to the Ball Game" web. (page 9)
- Create a baseball vocabulary chart.

Lesson 2
- Reread the story, taking note of rhythm and meter. Create a list of rhyming words. (page 6, Enjoying the Book)
- Write a sports review titled The Big Game in Mudville. (page 7, Enjoying the Book)
- Play spelling word baseball. (page 42)
- Begin a story-elements flip book suggested on page 6, Enjoying the Book.

Lesson 3
- Act out the story. (page 7, Extending the Book)

Lesson 3 (cont.)
- Draft descriptive paragraphs.
- Play baseball vocabulary concentration. (pages 10 and 11)
- Sing "Take Me Out to the Ball Game." (page 7, Extending the Book)

Lesson 4
- Read orally and then compare and contrast "Casey's Daughter at the Bat" with *Casey at the Bat*. (See *American Sports Poems*, compiled by R. R. Knudson and May Swenson (Orchard Books, Watts, 1988.)
- Complete "Y" Graph. (page 12)

Lesson 5
- Play a class baseball game. (page 7, Extending the Book)
- Create a baseball equipment man. (pages 13 and 14)
- Make pennants for favorite sports.

Overview of Activities

Setting the Stage

1. To stimulate interest in your *Sports Thematic Unit*, wear a baseball jersey and carry a baseball bat or a glove and a ball. Have the students predict what the new unit of study is going to be about. Write their predictions on chart paper.

2. Create an atmosphere of sports by allowing the students to bring in sports related items to display in a certain area of the room. (Some suggestions include trophies, posters, baseball cards, autographs, pennants, sports equipment, etc.)

3. In cooperative teams, have the students brainstorm what they know about sports and what they would like to know; at the end of the unit they can brainstorm what they have learned about sports. Have them write their responses on a KWL (**K**now **W**ould like to know, **L**earned) chart.

4. Prior to reading the story, have the students participate in a brainstorming activity about baseball games by completing the "Take Me Out to the Ball Game" writing web on page 9. Then have them write descriptive paragraphs about a baseball game, using the brainstorming worksheet provided. To help create some excitement about the unit, you may want to allow time for the students to share some of their personal experiences related to baseball games.

5. Make a graph of favorite sports in your class. Take a class poll to determine what each class member's favorite sport is. Record the information on a chart on the chalkboard, using tally marks for duplicated favorites. Have your students take the information on the chalkboard and design a graph using the information. Allow each student to share his or her graph. Use the activity on page 54 as a guide. You can extend this activity by taking a survey of other people in your school and graphing those results. Display the results of the graph in a visible location in your school. Prior to beginning, you may want to review the various types of graphs and show samples of each type.

Enjoying the Book

1. Have students preview and predict what the story will be about by looking at the front and back covers of the book. Ask the students if they know what a ballad is. After predictions are made, read the book straight through for enjoyment.

2. Read the story through a second time, taking note of the rhythm and meter of the story. Generate a list of rhyming words that appear throughout the story.

3. Discuss the elements of the story—*setting, characters, problem, events, ending,* and *mood*. Ask questions such as these:
   • What was the setting of the story? (Where and when did it take place?)
   • Who were the characters in the story?
   • What was the main problem in the story?
   • What are some of the important events that took place during the story?
   • What happened at the end of the story?
   • What was the mood of the story? Did the mood change?

   Use these story elements to create a flip book. Have the students write the answers to these questions in complete sentences on the flip book. Allow them to illustrate each element.

Overview of Activities *(cont.)*

Enjoying the Book *(cont.)*

4. Write a sports review of the big game in Mudville. Have the students pretend they are writing the review for the newspaper. Read some examples of sports reviews from a local paper to help them get started. Provide some stationery for the final copy. You may want to display the writing on a bulletin board entitled "The Big Game in Mudville."

Extending the Book

1. Have the students act out the story. Choose different students to be Casey, the umpire, the sister, the two batters who get hits, and the crowd. Reread the story aloud and let the students act as you read. Simple props such as a bat, gloves, baseball caps, and popcorn for the crowd will enhance the acting. You may want to have someone videotape the students after they have practiced a few times. They will love seeing themselves on TV after the play.

2. Write descriptive paragraphs about a real or an imaginary baseball adventure. As a prewriting activity, make a web to allow the students to generate their ideas.

3. Have a class baseball game. Use a plastic ball and bat for safety reasons. Divide your class into two teams. Go over the rules to the game. Enlist some parent volunteers to serve as umpires. You may also want to enlist some parents to serve hot dogs and soft drinks after the big game!

4. Play baseball concentration. See the directions and concentration cards on pages 10 and 11. Some blank baseball concentration cards and some extension activities have been provided for you.

5. Sing the song "Take Me Out to the Ball Game," lyrics written by Jack Northworth and music written by Albert Von Tilzer.

6. Construct a baseball equipment man as an art project. Use baseball-shaped patterns on pages 13 and 14 to create a baseball player. Take a large shape of a baseball bat and let that be the body. Use four smaller sized baseball bat patterns as arms and legs. Connect them to the body, using paper fasteners. Use a large baseball shape as a head. Glue the head to the body. Use four smaller-sized baseball patterns as hands and feet. Use the smallest-sized baseball bat patterns as fingers and toes. Glue these onto the hands and feet. Finish the project by adding a baseball hat to the head. This art project is sure to be a big hit!

7. Read the poem "Casey's Daughter at the Bat" written by Al Graham and found in the book *American Sports Poems*, compiled by R. R. Knudson and May Swenson (Orchard Books, Watts, 1988). Make a "Y" graph to compare and contrast Casey's daughter to Casey. A reproducible worksheet of the "Y" graph activity is found on page 12.

8. Have the students imagine that they are Casey. Have them write paragraphs about how they feel at the beginning of the game, during the middle of the game, and at the end of the game.

Overview of Activities *(cont.)*

Extending the Book *(cont.)*

9. Bring in a Polaroid camera, a baseball jersey, and some baseball equipment. Allow each student to try on the jersey and pose in a baseball position—for example, *a pitcher's stance, a catcher's position, a batting stance,* or a *fielder catching a fly ball.* Take the students' pictures and display them in your classroom. You may want the students to write a make-believe story about what is occurring in the picture. You may also want to let them use a tape recorder and have them be sports announcers describing the events in the picture.

10. Play spelling word bingo. Give each student a blank bingo sheet. Have the students write their sporty spelling words at random in the blanks. Then have the spelling words written on small strips of paper and placed in a container. Allow the students to take turns drawing and calling out the spelling words until someone calls bingo. Use the blank sports bingo sheet on page 47.

11. Develop a sports trivia game. Research the history of various sports. This would be a good cooperative learning project. Use the information to create a game similar to Trivial Pursuit. Make up questions based on cooperative team research. Use the questions in your game.

12. Play sports-around-the-world. Locate on a map the countries where various sports originated. Label the locations with sticky notes. Create flags of the various countries. On one side of the flag put a symbol of the sport. Have the other side resemble the country's flag. Use the world map provided on page 48 as a visual organizer for your information.

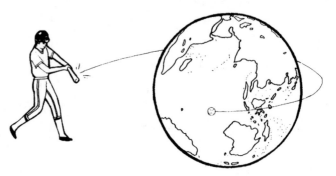

13. Compare sports equipment shapes. Have each student bring in one piece of sports equipment from home. Make a picto-graph of the equipment that is brought in by actually laying the equipment in rows or columns on the floor. Have the class develop labels for the x and y axis of your picto-graph. Write these labels on sentence strips and have students place them on the correct axis.

14. Use a newspaper to gather numerical information about sports. Use the information you find to create meaningful word problems about sports. Have the students locate the lowest and the highest numbers in the sports section of the paper. Have students list all the numbers they find on one page. Then have them order the numbers from the least to the greatest or the greatest to the least.

15. Make a big book of the various ways numbers are used in sports—numbers on uniforms, counting bases, scores, averages, salaries, etc. Have each student create a big book page that describes a specific way that numbers are used in a certain sport. Allow each student to illustrate his or her page of the big book.

16. Use the various point systems in certain sports to create word problems. For example, in football each touchdown is worth six points. If the Atlanta Falcons scored four touchdowns and no extra points, what was their final score? (4 x 6 = 24 points.)

"Take Me Out to the Ball Game"

Brainstorm words and phrases that describe a baseball game. Record your ideas near the appropriate baseball bat on the web below.

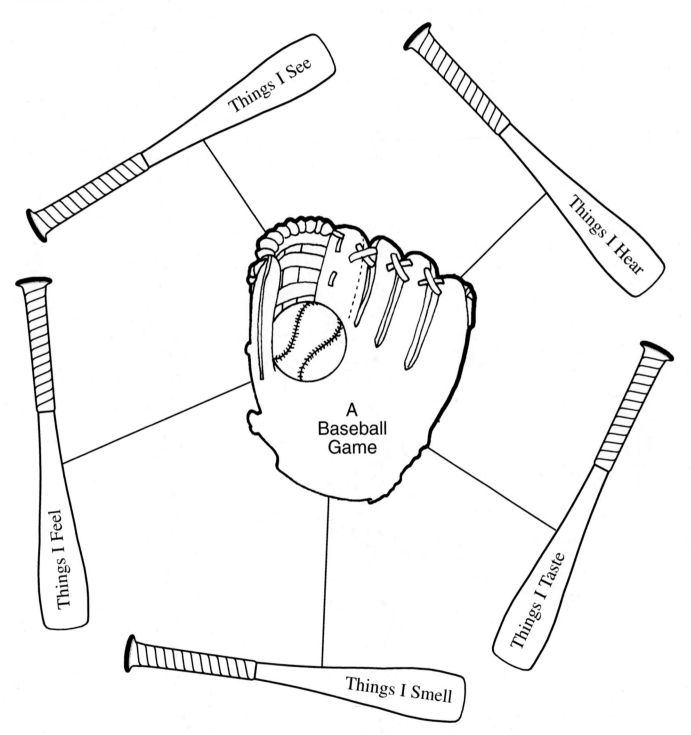

Extension Activity: Write a descriptive paragraph about a baseball game, using the words and phrases above. Remember to include a topic sentence.

Baseball Concentration

Directions for Creating the Game

Choose some of the new or difficult vocabulary words found in the story *Casey at the Bat* and have a "look-it-up-in-the-dictionary" contest. Put the students in pairs or cooperative teams. Give each group a dictionary. Show them a vocabulary word from the story. (You may want to write the words on large cards or on an overhead projector so the students are able to see the spelling of the word.) Allow the team that finds the word first to share the definition with the class. Have someone in each team record the definition of the word on a piece of paper. After all the vocabulary words have been located and recorded, have each pair of students create a concentration game. Use a baseball concentration card to write the words and the definitions on. The word should be written on one baseball concentration card and the definition on a separate card. Then, give the students some time to play their game.

How to Play

Have the students place the cards face down. Each student should then take a turn drawing the concentration cards, trying to match a word with the correct definition. The student who matches the most words to the definitions is the winner.

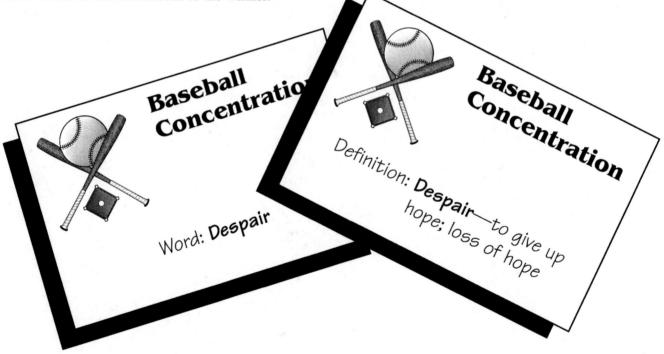

Extensions

1. These cards could also be used to play a game of Go Fish. Shuffle the cards and deal each player five cards. Each student takes turns asking another student for the match to either a definition or a word. If the student asked does not have the match, he or she says "Go fish," and the student asking then draws a card from the leftover cards. The object is to match the most definitions with words. The winner is the student with the most matches.

2. Save the cards and add to them throughout the sports unit. Use them to play a jeopardy-type game at the end of your sports theme. Divide your students into teams and award points for the first team who can give the correct definition for a word.

Baseball Concentration Cards

Baseball Concentration	**Baseball Concentration**
Baseball Concentration	**Baseball Concentration**
Baseball Concentration	**Baseball Concentration**
Baseball Concentration	**Baseball Concentration**

"Y" Graph

Directions

Record on the "Y" graph your ideas about how "Casey at the Bat" and "Casey's Daughter at the Bat" are alike and different. This graph will help you to compare and contrast these two pieces of literature.

"Casey at the Bat"

What Are
Their
Differences?

**"Casey's Daughter
at the Bat"**

How Are They Alike?

Baseball Equipment Man

Use the following patterns to create a baseball player. Use the largest baseball bat pattern as your baseball player's body. Use the medium-size baseball bats as arms and legs. The largest baseball pattern is the head of your baseball player. The smaller baseball patterns are the hands and feet. The toes and fingers of your baseball equipment man should be made from the smallest baseball bat patterns. All of these pieces should be connected using paper fasteners. Finish the project by adding a baseball hat to the head. You may want to use your favorite baseball team's emblem.

Baseball Equipment Man *(cont.)*

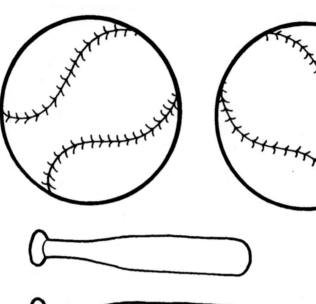
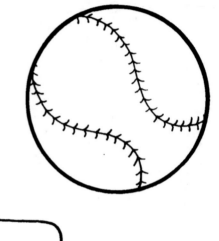
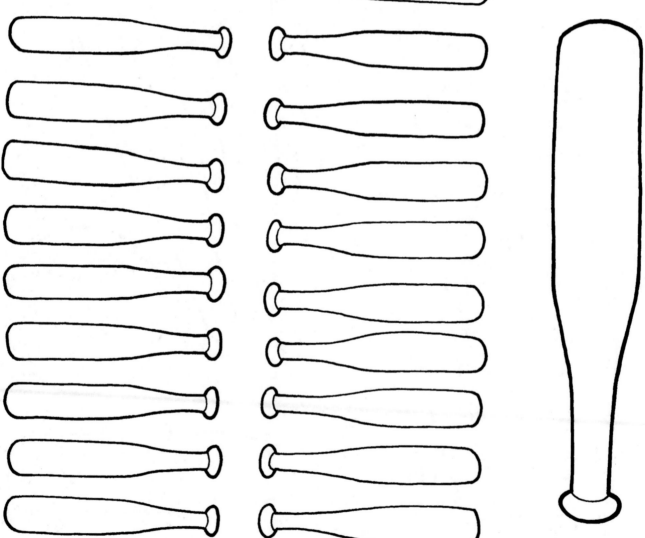

The Greatest Sports Stories Never Told

by Bruce Nash and Allan Zullo

Summary

The Greatest Sports Never Told is a book filled with 34 true stories about some unbelievable moments that have occurred in sports. The authors of this book used newspapers and "dusty collections from the sports hall of fame" to compile stories that depict "accounts of phenomenal feats, amazing courage, incredible incidents, and wonderful sportsmanship." Specifically, this book contains short nonfiction sports stories about Olympic athletes, baseball, football, boxing, horse racing, basketball, track and field, bowling, soccer, golf, and stock car racing. Students of all ages will enjoying reading and hearing these sports stories.

Because of the wide variety of sports that this book covers, it should be easy to integrate the sports that are of most interest to your students. Suggested activities for some of the sports stories are provided.

Sample Plan

Lesson 1
- Make a sports collage. (page 16, Setting the Stage)
- Begin the Sports ABC book. (page 41)
- Read "Pa's Promise" on pages 33–35.
- Use the sample bowling score and a plastic bowling set to practice keeping score on the bowling score sheet provided. (page 19)

Lesson 2
- Go on your class field trip to the bowling alley. (page 16, Setting the Stage)
- Create a class book, "Our Adventures in Bowling." (page 16, Setting the Stage)
- Chart bowling vocabulary words.

Lesson 3
- Read "The Olympics' First Champion" on pages 53–55.
- Begin the Sports Time Line. (pages 59–62)
- Complete a Venn Diagram: Summer/Winter Olympics.
- Locate Greece on the map.

Lesson 4
- Read "The Olympics' Wackiest Runner" on pages 73–74.
- Do the Sports Biography on page 20.
- Make a Sports Trivia game in cooperative teams. (pages 24 and 25)
- Continue building the Sports Time Line. (pages 59–62)

Lesson 5
- Read "When Winning Takes a Back Seat" on pages 91 and 92.
- Discuss good sportsmanship.
- Create The Sports Edition about your class. (page 44)
- Send home the Sporting Goods Extravaganza homework. (page 56)
- Complete building the Sports Time Line. (pages 59–62)

Overview of Activities

Setting the Stage

1. Set the mood by having the students create picture collages of various sports events. Include exciting headlines as well as photographs. Encourage the students to use magazines and newspapers when creating their collages. Display the collages in your classroom and use them as guides for a class discussion on how sports stories are contrived.

2. Adventures in Bowling—Plan a class field trip to a local bowling alley. Take a Polaroid camera with you and take a picture of each student bowling. Use the pictures to have the students write a "great sports story" about themselves as bowlers. Publish the stories in a class book entitled "Adventures in Bowling". Discuss with your students the fact that many exciting sports stories are never shared with other people. This will provide a wonderful opportunity for you to introduce *The Greatest Sports Stories Never Told* to your students.

3. Sports Search—Have students research their favorite sports. Encourage them to use encyclopedias and other reference materials to research various sports. Ask students to find out where the sport they have chosen was originally played, what the rules are, and who are some of the famous people related to the sport. Distribute copies of the Sports Search on page 43 for students to complete. Ask students to share their research with the class. Encourage your students to use visual aids as part of their presentations. Have students save their research information in their language arts portfolio for the culminating activity at the end of the unit.

4. Favorite Sport Diorama—Make a diorama of your favorite sport. See page 71.

5. Read "The Bench-Warmer Who Won the Rose Bowl." Discuss with your students how points are awarded to teams in a football game. Complete the Football Frolics activity on page 23.

6. Sports Story Web—Have students read a book about a famous person in sports. Have them use the web on page 45 to assist them in organizing the information they learn. Have them use the information to write a paragraph or book report. Make a person-shaped book to illustrate and display the writing. Note the illustration of how to create a person-shaped book. Attach student writing inside the flaps on the body. Add head, hands, legs, and other features.

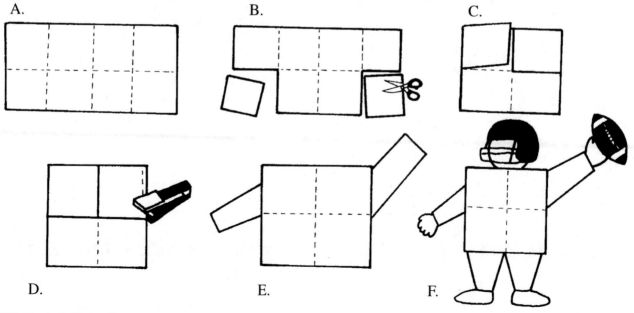

A.   B.   C.

D.   E.   F.

Overview of Activities *(cont.)*

Enjoying the Book

1. It is recommended that you read aloud a short story from this book to your class each day during the unit.

2. Read the story selection "Pa's Promise" prior to your trip to the bowling alley. Use the sample bowling score sheet on page 19 and sharpen your students' math skills by teaching them how to keep score. Also, introduce some bowling vocabulary words such as *strike, spare, gutter ball, frame, league,* and *tournament.* Since this particular story depicts the grandfather as a hero, you might to have your students write about their heroes.

3. The Sports Edition—Have your students work in cooperative teams to create a mock sports edition of a newspaper. Allow them to include real sports stories about themselves in their sports edition. Help them decide what to write about by creating a class generated list of ideas. Ask questions that lead your students to think about things that have happened to them while participating in a particular sport. You might ask questions such as these: Have you ever participated in or watched a sports event in which something unusual or unique happened? What is the most exciting game you have ever been a part of, and why was it so exciting? What was your greatest moment in sports? Use page 44 to make a newspaper page.

4. Use the story "The Olympics' Wackiest Runner" as a springboard to discuss the Olympic Games. Before reading the story, brainstorm with your students any information that they know about the Olympic Games. Ask them to discuss what they know about the history of the Olympics, about modern day Olympics, about Olympic awards and ceremonies, about great Olympic champions, and about how people make the Olympic teams. Read the story and enjoy!

5. The story selection entitled "The Olympics' First Champion" lends itself to numerous classroom activities. Some that you might choose from include creating an Olympic time line by researching the history of the Olympic Games. Use the Venn diagram on page 21 to compare and contrast the winter and summer Olympic games. Study the Greek culture.

6. The story "When Winning Took a Back Seat" provides a wonderful opportunity to discuss the concept of good sportsmanship. After reading the story, your students may wish to discuss some ways to show good sportsmanship in various sporting events. Your class may also want to discuss the notion that winning isn't everything.

7. Create a fact cube about a certain sport. Write six factual sentences about a specific sport. Write and illustrate each fact on the cube pattern on page 22. Fold the cube pattern and glue it together.

8. Sports Postcard Activity—Send a postcard to a friend telling about your favorite sport. Use the postcard pattern on page 49.

9. Sports Are Where the Action Is—This is a perfect unit to introduce or reinforce the concept of the action verb. Begin by showing various pictures of people interacting in sports. Have students brainstorm a list of actions they see taking place. Write the list on the chalkboard or on chart paper. In cooperative groups have the students go on a scavenger hunt around your school, searching for more action words. Use the words to make a class big book or a cooperative group book of the action words they find. Have them illustrate each action word and put it in a sentence. Let them share their books with students in other classes. Use activity page 46 during the scavenger hunt. (This would also be a great time to play the Sports Charades game listed next.)

Overview of Activities *(cont.)*

Enjoying the Book *(cont.)*

10. Sports Charades—Play sports charades with your students. Allow students to act out or mime their favorite sports for the class. You may want to use some of the sports listed on page 41 if your students have difficulty thinking of sports to act out. Let your other students try to guess the sports being acted out.

11. Sports Guide-Words Chain—Have students make vocabulary chains about a certain sport. At the top of the chain use the shape of a piece of equipment for that particular sport. On the links of the chain students will write various vocabulary words that relate to the sport. Have the student write the vocabulary word in the center of the chain. On either side of the vocabulary word the student will write the dictionary guide words which would help locate that word in a dictionary. Connect the links to the shape in alphabetical order. Hang the chains from the ceiling to create a festive mood in your classroom. Have a contest to see who can have the most links to their chain!

Extending the Book

1. Write sports biographies about favorite sports figures. Use the Sports Biography book report form on page 20 as a guide.

2. Create a big book of your students' greatest moments in sports. Use the guidelines on page 50 for help.

3. Play sports trivia with your students. Use activity pages 24 and 25 for this activity. Design a box in which to store the class trivia questions. Have your students write one sports trivia question a day on the sports trivia question strips on page 24. Deposit the strips into the trivia box. Begin each day with a trivia question from the box. Have one student choose a question and read it aloud. Have the other students record their answers on the Sports Trivia Activity Sheet (page 25). Discuss the answer with your class after all students have had time to respond. Use these sports trivia questions to play the cooperative game suggestion on page 57.

4. Sports Award—Design an award for a famous sports personality or for a friend in your classroom. (page 70)

5. Sports Pennants—Make a pennant for your favorite sports or team. Display the pennants on the wall.

6. Sports Collage—Make an exercise/sports collage. Use words as well as pictures.

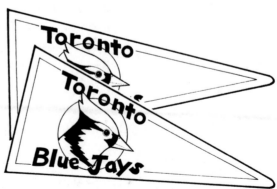

7. Sporting Goods Extravaganza—As a homework assignment have the students visit a local sporting goods store and find out the prices of different pieces of sports equipment. Have them record their data. Use the information to create word problems to solve together in class. Make sure you give the students an adequate period of time to gather their data. Also, use the information to compare prices and determine the most economical purchases.

Adventures in Bowling

Bowling is an indoor sport played on a polished wooden floor called an *alley*. It can be played by individuals or in teams. The player(s) roll balls down the alley, attempting to knock down 10 wooden pins.

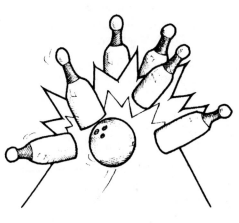

The score of the bowling game is determined by the number of pins knocked down in 10 frames. Each bowler bowls two times during each frame. Each pin that is knocked down counts as one point. If all the pins are knocked down on the first ball, it is called a *strike* and an X is placed in the first small square on the score sheet. If the bowler is able to knock down all the pins in two rolls, it is called a *spare* and a / is placed in the second small square of the score sheet. When scoring a strike, the bowler receives 10 points for the strike, plus the total of the next two rolls. When scoring a spare, the bowler receives 10 points for the spare plus the number of pins knocked down in the next roll. A perfect score in bowling is 300 points.

Example:

	1st roll	2nd roll		1st roll	spare								

| | **2** | **5** | | **7** | / | | **3** | **5** | | **X** | | | **3** | **5** |
| **7** | total of rolls | | **20** | previous total + 10 + next roll | | **28** | | | **46** | previous total + 10 + next 2 rolls | | **54** | |

frame 1   frame 2   frame 3   frame 4   frame 5

Sample Score Sheet:

NAME	1	2	3	4	5	6	7	8	9	10	TOTAL
Bowler 1											
Bowler 2											
Bowler 3											
Bowler 4											

You can create your own version of a bowling alley by using 10 empty 2-liter soda bottles and a medium-sized ball. Practice rolling the ball and knocking down the pins (bottles). Use the sample score sheet provided to record your score.

Sports Biography

Directions: Read a biography about a famous sports figure. Use this sheet to help you gather information about this person. Record the information you find in the correct spaces. If you need more space, use the back of this page.

1. Famous sports figure:

   _____

2. Title and author of the book:

   _____

   _____

3. Sport(s) involved:

   _____

   _____

   _____

4. Why is this person famous?

   _____

   _____

   _____

   _____

5. Why did you choose this person?

   _____

   _____

6. Write three interesting facts you learned about this person:

   _____

   _____

7. Write a brief summary of the book you read.

   _____

   _____

   _____

   _____

   _____

   _____

   _____

   _____

   _____

   _____

   _____

   _____

   _____

   _____

   Report Written By:

   _____

Summer and Winter Olympics

Directions: Use the Venn diagram below to compare and contrast the Summer Olympics and the Winter Olympics. List words or phrases that apply only to the Summer Olympics in the Summer Olympics circle. List words or phrases that apply only to the Winter Olympics in the Winter Olympics circle. In the middle section list words and phrases that apply to both Olympic games.

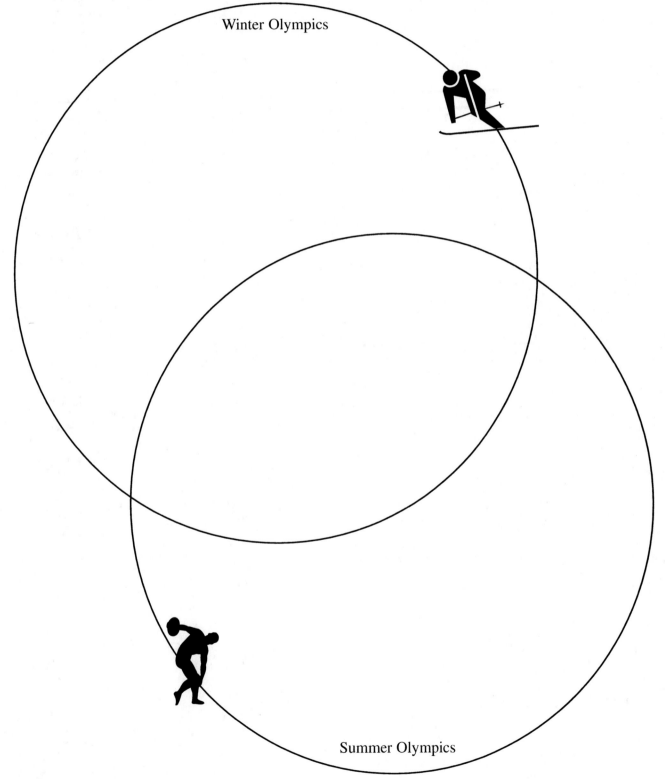

Fact Cube

Directions: Create a fact cube about a certain sport. Write six factual sentences about a specific sport. Write and illustrate each fact on the cube pattern below. Fold the cube pattern and glue it together. Trade your fact cube with a friend and learn new information about a different sport.

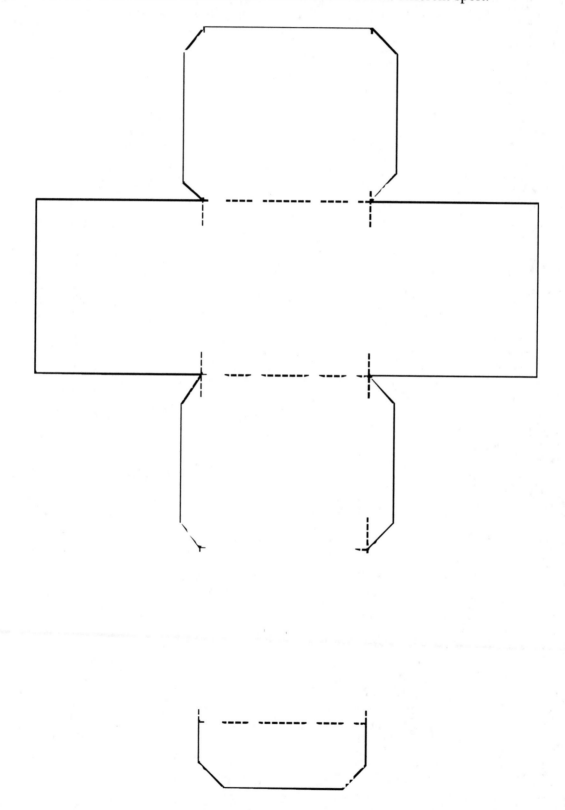

Football Frolics

Use the following football scoreboard to solve the problems below. Keep in mind that some of the problems will require more than one mathematical procedure.

Football Scoreboard		
touchdowns	=	6 points each
field goals	=	3 points each
safeties	=	2 points each
conversions—by kick	=	1 point each
conversions—by pass or run	=	2 points each

1. The Atlanta Falcons played the San Francisco 49ers on Monday night. The Falcons scored three touchdowns, two extra points, and a safety. The 49ers scored two touchdowns, two extra points and two safeties. What was the final score of the game?

2. The Dallas Cowboys and the Washington Redskins were tied at the half of their football game. The score was 21 to 21. Dallas scored three more touchdowns and three more extra points. Washington scored three more touchdowns, one extra point, and a safety. What was the final score of the game? Who won?

3. The New Orleans Saints upset the Tampa Bay Buccaneers last weekend by beating them 32 to 0. Use the scoreboard to come up with a possible score distribution for the Saints' points.

4. Pittsburgh played Denver in a play-off game. Denver had three two-point conversions during the game, four touchdowns, three extra points, and a safety. Pittsburgh fumbled once, scored two touchdowns, two extra points, and three safeties. What was each team's final score?

5. The Cleveland Browns and the St. Louis Cardinals had a final football game score of 36 to 26. Cleveland scored three touchdowns, two extra points, and two field goals. Did Cleveland win or lose this football game?

Bonus: Create your own word problem about your favorite football teams. Use the scoreboard above to assist you. Have a friend try to solve your problem.

Sports Trivia

Name: _____

Sports Trivia Question: _____

_____

_____

Write the answer to your question on the back.

Remember to make sure your sentences are complete. Ask a friend to check.

Name: _____

Sports Trivia Question: _____

_____

_____

Write the answer to your question on the back.

Remember to make sure your sentences are complete. Ask a friend to check.

Name: _____

Sports Trivia Question: _____

_____

_____

Write the answer to your question on the back.

Remember to make sure your sentences are complete. Ask a friend to check.

Name: _____

Sports Trivia Question: _____

_____

_____

Write the answer to your question on the back.

Remember to make sure your sentences are complete. Ask a friend to check.

24

Sports Trivia Activity Sheet

Use this activity sheet to record your answers to the sports trivia questions asked each day. Remember to write your answers as complete sentences.

1. _____
_____
2. _____
_____
3. _____
_____
4. _____
_____
5. _____
_____
6. _____
_____
7. _____
_____
8. _____
_____
9. _____
_____
10. _____
_____

The Winning Stroke

by Matt Christopher

Summary

This is the story of Jerry Grayson, who turns to swimming as a way to heal a baseball injury—a broken leg—so that he can return to his favorite sport on the diamond. He doesn't suspect that he will come to like swimming as a sport, especially since he is not really skilled or trained as a swimmer. The challenges, his shortcomings, and the stiff competition discourage him at first, but his friends and family along with his own competitive spirit help him to achieve success. He learns that he must master the techniques of the *crawl*, the *breaststroke*, the *backstroke*, and the *butterfly* to be an all-around swimmer. To be competitive, he must learn the fine points of *starting, racing turns, dry-land exercises, self-control,* and *concentration,* among other things. Students will enjoy the good humor, anticipation, and character building that go into this exciting Matt Christopher sports story.

Sample Plan

Lesson 1
- Create a swimming vocabulary chart.
- Read Chapters 1–3 on pages 3–32. Discuss Jerry's accident—how it happened, what a "fractured tibia and fibula" means, and what Jerry's therapy is going to be. Ask students to explain how Jerry feels about being in the pool when the real swimming team comes in to practice.
- Make a class book of swimming stories.

Lesson 2
- Read Chapters 4–6 on pages 33–67. Discuss Jerry's feelings when he finishes behind Tanya. How does he react to the criticism from Wayne? Why does Jerry's mother suggest that he is "not used to learning anything new when it comes to sports—any sport." Ask the students to tell how Tanya and Tony get Jerry to ask the coach if he can go out for the team.
- Complete the Crazy Swimming Relays activity. (page 27)
- Chart swimming safety rules.

Lesson 3
- Read Chapters 7–9 on pages 68–109. Discuss how Jerry felt after coming in last in his first real race. What excuse did he try to use with the coach? What is the real lesson Jerry learns when he realizes that a "natural stroke" is not enough? "As he got to know them, the other members of the team were generous with their praise and their help"—what lesson does Jerry learn from this?
- Read and discuss "Different Strokes for Different Folks." (page 34)

- Complete the Why Exercise? activity. (page 29)
- Take a field trip to an indoor pool.

Lesson 4
- Do the brainstorming activity "Animals That Swim." (page 28, Extending the Book)
- Read Chapters 10–12 on pages 110–140.
- Discuss the false start and disqualification in the 500 yard freestyle race. Discuss how Jerry's family shows good humor by reminding him of his mistakes—throwing his mitt, striking out, and swinging the bat so hard he almost knocked himself out.
- Do the "Hearts in Motion" activity. (pages 65–66)

Lesson 5
- Read Chapters 13–15 on pages 141–168. Discuss the important thing Jerry learns from Tanya (the relaxed pause before starting) and, of course, the even more important lesson for us all—*that we can learn from anybody if only we are willing.* What lesson did Jerry learn from Tony, who came over to congratulate him, even though he was "possibly eliminated from the one event he wanted to do well in." Discuss the overall theme of *The Winning Stroke*—individual hard work, good humor, diligence, and helping one another can result in success and powerful feeings of accomplishment.
- Write poems about swimming.
- Complete the Venn diagram comparing and contrasting swimming in a lake, a pool, and the ocean. (page 30)

Overview of Activities

Setting the Stage

1. Swimming goggles, flippers, a beach towel, and other swimming gear will help to set the stage and generate some excitement when introducing this book. Display or wear some of these items before reading the book to your class. Elicit some discussion about swimming as a sport.

2. Make a chart of swimming vocabulary words by brainstorming as a class. Discuss the meanings of the words. Display the list in your classroom during your sports unit. Add words to the list as your unit continues.

3. Make a class book of true swimming stories.

Enjoying the Book

1. *The Winning Stroke* contains many exciting suggestions for the reader to consider. It introduces the reader to many swimming skills along with powerful lessons for building character. If possible, plan a field trip to an indoor pool in your community. Arrange for a lifeguard to be present and allow your students to try out some of the swimming strokes mentioned in the book. Before your field trip, have your students work in cooperative learning teams to create a new water game to play in the pool. Suggest that they give their game a catchy title and some rules. Give them an opportunity to teach the class their game. (If an indoor pool is not available, you could play a land version of each water game.)

2. Compare and contrast swimming in a lake, a pool, and the ocean. Use the Venn diagram provided for your students on page 30 to record their information.

3. Use the Swimming with the Alphabet activity on page 31 to review alphabetizing skills with your students. As an extension your class could brainstorm a list of animals that swim. Use the list to continue to practice alphabetizing skills. Have each student conduct research on one of the animals from your list to create an "Animals That Swim" nonfiction class book.

4. Crazy Swimming Relays—Practice those swimming strokes by having some class swimming relays. Your students will love dressing up in goggles, flippers, and flotation devices and participating in some crazy swimming relays on land. Teach your students how to use a stop-watch during these relays so they can record their times. Use the data to create a graph of each person's time in each event. Be sure to take some pictures. This is sure to be an event they will not soon forget!

5. Create a list of class-generated verbs and adjectives that describe swimming. Use the list to write poems about various swimming strokes, water sports, water games, etc. Illustrate your poems and display them in your classroom.

Overview of Activities *(cont.)*

Enjoying the Book *(cont.)*

6. Discuss safety rules for swimming. Make a chart to display these rules in your classroom. Some suggestions include "Swim with others" and "Wait 30 minutes after eating before swimming."

7. Use the activity sheet entitled Daily Dietary Needs on page 32 to teach your students the basic food groups and the recommended daily servings from each group. Then on page 33 have your students keep a weekly record of the foods they eat in each food group. Discuss the results from keeping the weekly record. You may want to have your students keep this record for more than one week to see if their eating habits improve.

8. A variety of strokes are used in swimming, each requiring different motions. Use the activity page entitled Different Strokes for Different Folks to teach your students the major swimming strokes (page 34). You may want to go over this page together prior to doing the swimming relay activity suggested above.

Extending the Book

1. Participate in a class study on water pollution. Discuss the causes and effects of water pollution on public lakes and rivers in your area. Invite a speaker from a water treatment plant to visit your class and talk to your students.

2. Have a class beach day to culminate your study on swimming. Be sure your students bring their beach towels and sunglasses for their day at the beach. Beach music and games will enhance your beach day festivities.

3. Brainstorm a list of animals that swim. Participate in a class study on fish, whales, and porpoises. Look at the body structure of fish, whales, and porpoises, and discuss why they are able to swim so well.

4. Create four-page pamphlets about swimming. On the front flap have the students write titles for their pamphlets. On the first inside flap have your students write brief paragraphs about swimming. On the second inside flap have them list some of the various places people can enjoy the sport of swimming. On the final flap have them include a list of swimming safety rules. Remind your students that pamphlets are usually used as a way of advertising something. Encourage them to provide colorful illustrations.

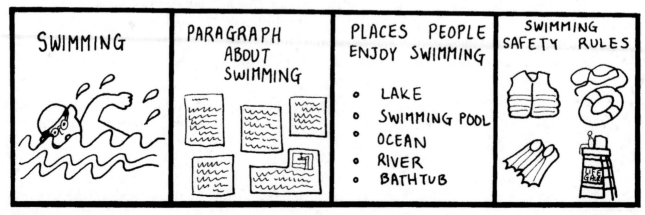

Overview of Activities *(cont.)*

Extending the Book *(cont.)*

5. Why Exercise?—Reinforce the concepts of proper nutrition and exercise. Discuss the values of exercising for fun and for health purposes. Use the chart on page 63 entitled Why Exercise? to create a list of the types of exercise, reasons to exercise, and good exercise habits.

6. Exercise Record—Have students keep a weekly exercise record. Record the type of exercise and/or sport participated in and the length of time it was practiced. An activity page for recording weekly exercise has been provided on page 64. Have your students fill in their names in the blank.

7. Flex Those Muscles!—Study about the muscles of the body. Help students learn what it means to make a muscle expand and contract. Use page 67 as a guide.

8. Hearts in Motion—Study about the heart and how it functions before, during, and after exercise. Discuss heart rate and teach students how to take a pulse. Learn the parts of the heart. Use pages 65 and 66 to assist you.

9. Read the book *The Magic School Bus® Inside the Human Body* written by Joanna Cole and illustrated by Bruce Degen. Create a large reproduction of the inside of the human body. On note cards or sentence strips, have the students label the important parts inside the body. Review what the function is of each part. Display the labeled body on your classroom wall. Follow up this activity with a discussion on what our bodies do with the energy we get from food. A sample bulletin board display (TCM #1775) produced by Teacher Created Materials appears below.

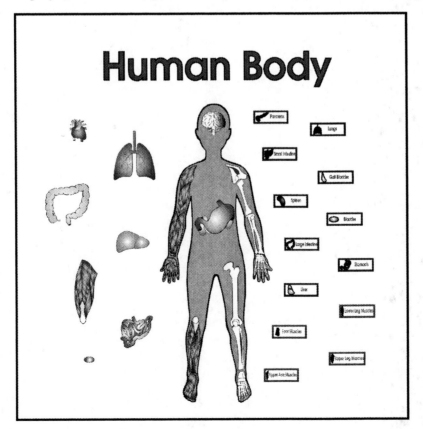

10. Make an energy trail mix to enjoy as a snack.

Swimming Venn Diagram

Use the Venn diagram to compare and contrast swimming in a lake, a pool, and the ocean. Remember that to *compare* means to tell how things are alike and *to contrast* means to tell how they are different. Record your thoughts and ideas on the Venn diagram below.

Swimming with the Alphabet

Use your alphabetizing skills to place the following swimming words in alphabetical order. You may have to look at the first, second, or third letters to determine the order of some of the words.

Swimming Words				
backstroke	butterfly	swimsuit	pool	free-style
lifeguard	dive	cannonball	springboards	lanes
diving board	dog paddle	float	ocean	takeoff
glide	splash	lake	kick	breathing
breaststroke	twists	flips	plunge	medley

1. _____

2. _____

3. _____

4. _____

5. _____

6. _____

7. _____

8. _____

9. _____

10. _____

11. _____

12. _____

13. _____

14. _____

15. _____

16. _____

17. _____

18. _____

19. _____

20. _____

21. _____

22. _____

23. _____

24. _____

25. _____

Daily Dietary Needs

In all sports, including swimming and diving, it is important for people to eat the proper foods and the proper amounts of food. The following chart adapted from the *Dietary Guidelines for Americans* (United States Department of Agriculture Home and Garden Bulletin Number 32) lists the essential food groups and the number of servings children and adults should have in each group each day.

Food Groups	Recommended Servings per Day	
	Children	Adults
Grains (includes breads, cereals, pasta, rice, and potatoes)	at least 6 servings a day	6–11
Fruits	at least 2 servings a day	2–4
Vegetables	at least 3 servings a day	3–5
Meats/Meat Alternatives (includes fish, poultry, dry beans and peas, and eggs)	at least 2 servings a day	2–3
Milk/Dairy Products	at least 2 servings a day	men 2–3 women 3–4
Fats/Sweets (includes butter, margarines, oils, candy, cookies, cakes, and soft drinks)	only in moderation	only in moderation

Weekly Dietary Record

Dietary Intake for _____

Make a list of all the food you eat each day for one week. Use the Daily Dietary Needs activity page on page 32 to help you compare your intake with what your body actually needs.

Monday	Tuesday	Wednesday
Grains:_____ _____	Grains:_____ _____	Grains:_____ _____
Fruits: _____ _____	Fruits: _____ _____	Fruits: _____ _____
Vegetables: _____ _____	Vegetables: _____ _____	Vegetables: _____ _____
Meats: _____ _____	Meats: _____ _____	Meats: _____ _____
Milk/Dairy: _____ _____	Milk/Dairy: _____ _____	Milk/Dairy: _____ _____
Fats/Sweets: _____ _____	Fats/Sweets: _____ _____	Fats/Sweets: _____ _____

Thursday	Friday	Summary
Grains:_____ _____	Grains:_____ _____	Use your weekly food chart to answer the following questions: Did you get enough food in each of the food groups for each day? _____ _____
Fruits: _____ _____	Fruits: _____ _____	
Vegetables: _____ _____	Vegetables: _____ _____	
Meats: _____ _____	Meats: _____ _____	Which food group was the most difficult for you to meet your daily dietary needs? _____ _____
Milk/Dairy: _____ _____	Milk/Dairy: _____ _____	
Fats/Sweets: _____ _____	Fats/Sweets: _____ _____	

Different Strokes for Different Folks

Crawl

The crawl (also known as the free-style stroke) is used in all parts of the world. The swimmer is in a face-down position on top of the water. This stroke involves carrying one arm forward out of the water to a nearly full extension while the other arm is still below the surface of the water, making a pulling motion that propels the body forward through the water. At the same time the arms are moving, the feet are moving in a kicking motion. The swimmer's face is in the water until he or she needs to take a breath. Breathing is accomplished by turning the head to one side or the other.

Backstroke

The backstroke is similar to the crawl but is performed on the back. One arm is carried over the swimmer's head out of the water to prepare for the next stroke while the other arm in the water completes a forward-pulling motion. The swimmer alternates his or her feet to kick.

Breaststroke

The breaststroke requires the swimmer to use leg and arm movements at the same time. The swimmer's hands are brought together under the chest and pushed forward to full extension. They are then swept back to the sides, parallel to the body. From this position the arm movement is repeated. The legs perform a frog-type kick. Both legs are brought up with the knees bent and each leg turned out. The legs are then thrust back to a parallel line with the rest of the body.

Butterfly

The butterfly stroke is similar to the breaststroke. Arm and leg movements are performed at the same time. The main difference between the butterfly stroke and the breaststroke is that the arm movements occur above the water in the butterfly stroke. This stroke is the most physically challenging of all the swimming strokes.

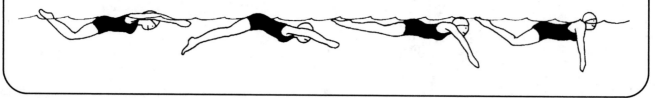

34

Sports Author Highlight—Matt Christopher

Biographical Information

Matt Christopher writes fiction books about sports for children. He was born on August 16, 1917, in Bath, Pennsylvania. He is the oldest of nine children. As a child he enjoyed playing games and playing baseball. He did not have the money to buy a ball and bat when he was a child, and until he could afford them he used tennis balls and broom handles.

At the age of 19, Matt Christopher signed a contract to play professional baseball for Smith Falls, Ontario, Canada, in the Canadian-American League. His career as a professional baseball player lasted only two months. After this he played semi-pro baseball and worked at odd jobs. Although baseball was his favorite sport, he also enjoyed playing football, basketball, and soccer.

Matt Christopher started writing when he was 14 years old. He wrote short stories, articles, and some poetry. At the age of 18 he won a short writing contest from *Writer's Digest*. The types of stories he wrote included articles for magazines (both adult and children's), sports stories, pulp detective stories, and science fiction stories. His favorite topic to write about now, however, is sports. He has written over 300 short stories and articles.

Before he writes a story or an article, he likes to research his topic. In 1979 he published his first book about motor sports. He did not know much about motor sports, but he wanted to write about them because they were popular at that time. He went to various motor sports events and interviewed the participants and the fans. He enjoyed the hands-on research he did before he wrote because he got involved in the excitement and thrill of the sport by experiencing it firsthand.

Mr. Christopher married his wife, Catherine, when he was 23 years old. He has raised a family of four children—Martin, Pamela, Dale, and Duane. He now lives in Rocky Hill, South Carolina, and has seven grandchildren.

Because his books contain so much sports excitement, children enjoy reading them. Most of his books also include some sort of lesson for life for a young person to relate to.

On the following page is a list of sports books written by Matt Christopher. His favorite book of all the ones he has written is *The Great Quarterback Switch*.

Sports Stories by Matt Christopher

(*The following titles are all published by Little, Brown & Co.*)

Baseball Flyhawk, 1995

Baseball Pals, 1990

The Basket Counts, 1991

Catch That Pass!, 1989

Catcher with a Glass Arm, 1985

Centerfield Ballhawk, 1994

Challenge at Second Base, 1992

The Counterfeit Tackle, 1990

Diamond Champs, 1990

Dirt Bike Racer, 1986

Dirt Bike Runaway, 1989

The Dog That Pitched a No-Hitter, 1993

The Dog That Stole Home, 1996

Face-Off, 1989

Fighting Tackle, 1996

Football Fugitive, 1988

The Fox Steals Home, 1985

The Great Quarterback Switch, 1991

Hard Drive to Short, 1991

The Hit-Away Kid, 1990

The Hockey Machine, 1992

Ice Magic, 1987

The Kid Who Only Hit Homers, 1986

Little Lefty, 1993

Long Shot for Paul, 1990

Long Stretch at First Base, 1993

Look Who's Playing First Base, 1987

The Lucky Baseball Bat, 1991

Man Out at First, 1995

Miracle at the Plate, 1989

Red-Hot Hightops, 1992

Run, Billy, Run, 1988

Shortstop from Tokyo, 1988

Skateboard Tough, 1994

Soccer Halfback, 1985

The Spy on Third Base, 1990

The Submarine Pitch, 1992

Supercharged Infield, 1994

Tackle Without a Team, 1993

Takedown, 1990

Tight End, 1991

Too Hot to Handle, 1991

Top Wing, 1991

Touchdown for Tommy, 1985

Tough to Tackle, 1987

Undercover Tailback, 1992

Wingman on Ice, 1993

The Winning Stroke, 1994

The Year Mom Won the Pennant, 1986

Zero's Slider, 1994

Author Study Ideas and Activities

Listed below are some ideas and activities to enhance an author study on Matt Christopher:

1. Set up an author highlight center in your classroom. Display Matt Christopher's name in large print. Reproduce a copy of the information about his life and have it on display at the center. Allow your students to make book jackets to resemble Matt Christopher's books. Provide copies of selected Matt Christopher stories for students to enjoy in your classroom.

2. Make a graph of the sports Matt Christopher has written about. Use the graph to draw conclusions about which sport is his favorite to write about.

3. Make sports bookmarks to use while reading Christopher's books.

4. Have the students work in cooperative teams to create a Fact-or-Opinion game about Matt Christopher's life and his works. Give each team an opportunity to read information about Matt Christopher. Have them make up fact-or-opinion game cards and a game board. On the cards have the students write a statement that is either a fact or an opinion. To play the game, players will take turns deciding whether the statement read is a fact or an opinion. If they get the correct answer, they get to move forward a certain number of spaces on the game board. If they answer incorrectly, they have to move back a space on the game board. The first player to finish wins the game.

5. Write letters to join the Matt Christopher Fan Club. Each student will need to send a self-addressed, stamped envelope (business-letter size) to:

> **Matt Christopher Fan Club**
> **34 Beacon Street**
> **Boston, MA 02108**

6. Select a Matt Christopher book to read aloud to your classroom during your sports study. You may want to read *The Year Mom Won the Pennant*, (Little, Brown & Co., 1986). Some activities you may use with this story include the following:

   • After you read chapter three, you may want to teach your students how to play chess. You could discuss the strategy and the problem-solving skills involved in the game.

   • In chapter three, also, one of the characters in the story is referred to as *Jabber* Kane. This nickname was given to this character for a specific reason. You may want to begin a discussion about nicknames and how people get them. Have the students write about any nicknames they have and why they were given those nicknames.

   • Throughout the story make a chart of baseball vocabulary words.

   • Discuss why the boys felt strange having a woman for a coach. Consider the different roles men and women take on in today's society compared to those roles when *The Year Mom Won the Pennant* was written. You may want to make a Venn diagram comparing now to then.

Fact-or-Opinion Game

Use the biographical information about Matt Christopher to create a game about the famous author. As a cooperative group, read the biographical information and write some sentences about Matt Christopher. Some of your sentences should be factual sentences. Other sentences should be opinion sentences about him.

For example:

A **factual sentence** you might use would be this:
> *Matt Christopher's wife is named Catherine.*

This is a true statement about Matt Christopher; therefore, it is a factual statement about him.

An **opinion sentence** you might use would be this:
> *Matt Christopher writes the best stories in the whole library.*

Although you may feel that this is a true statement, it is your opinion of Matt Christopher and may not be the same opinion that other people have.

After creating 16–20 fact-and-opinion cards about Matt Christopher, your team should design a game board for your game. Use your imaginations about what your game board will look like. You may want to draw a draft copy on scrap paper before you actually create it. The object of your game should be to advance around the game board by answering the fact-or-opinion game cards correctly. You may want to have a consequence for a wrong answer (for example: moving a game piece back two spaces).

Your team will also need to write some rules for your game and provide some game pieces. Use the game cards provided on page 39 to write your fact-or-opinion statements on.

Your team should be able to trade games with another team and be able to understand one another's directions, so proofread your rules carefully.

Below is a sample game board idea that you may want to use.

Fact-or-Opinion Game Cards

### Fact or Opinion? Determine whether the following statement is a fact or an opinion.	### Fact or Opinion? Determine whether the following statement is a fact or an opinion.
### Fact or Opinion? Determine whether the following statement is a fact or an opinion.	### Fact or Opinion? Determine whether the following statement is a fact or an opinion.
### Fact or Opinion? Determine whether the following statement is a fact or an opinion.	### Fact or Opinion? Determine whether the following statement is a fact or an opinion.
### Fact or Opinion? Determine whether the following statement is a fact or an opinion.	### Fact or Opinion? Determine whether the following statement is a fact or an opinion.

Matt Christopher Sports Graph

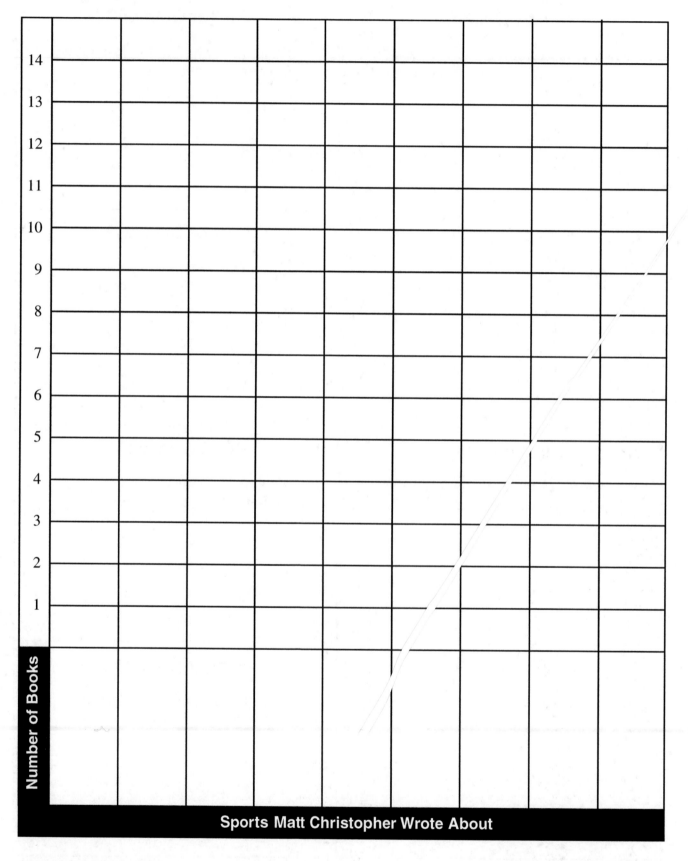

14
13
12
11
10
9
8
7
6
5
4
3
2
1

Number of Books

Sports Matt Christopher Wrote About

Language, Writing, and Poetry Activities

1. Have students write paragraphs about their favorite sport. Make a sports writing web to gather ideas for the paragraphs. Use the web to write draft copies. Have students edit their paragraphs and write final copies on sports-related stationery.

2. Write "how to" paragraphs—for example, "How to Play_____." Make a flip book to illustrate the steps to a certain sports skill or to tell the rules for playing a particular sport.

3. ABC Book—Make an alphabet book of sports. Include a brief description of each sport and an illustration. This would be a good team project. A sample listing of sports and sports-related words has been provided.

aerial sports	football	rowing
archery	golf	rugby
automobile racing	gymnastics	sailing
badminton	handball	shooting
baseball	hockey	skateboarding
basketball	horse racing	skating
birling	hurling	skiing
boating	ice hockey	skydiving
bobsledding	ice skating	soccer
boxing	jai alai	softball
bullfighting	kayaking	speedball
canoeing	lacrosse	surfing
cricket	martial arts	swimming
croquet	motorcycling	tennis
curling	mountaineering	tobogganing
cycling	orienteering	volleyball
dog racing	paddle tennis	water polo
diving	platform tennis	water-skiing
fencing	polo	weight lifting
field hockey	racquetball	wrestling
fishing	roller-skating	

4. Use sports-related words for spelling study. For example, basketball words might include *relay, rebound, free throw, shoot, basket, foul, pass, referee, goal,* and *points.* Set up spelling stations/centers to practice the spelling words. Some suggested stations/centers follow:

   a. Spelling Word Hangman—Use the spelling words to play hangman. Have a student choose a spelling word and draw a hangman symbol on the chalkboard. Let the other students try to guess the letters of the word. The first student to guess the word gets to choose the next word.

   b. Sporty Spelling Word Search—Give each student a blank word search sheet. Have the students write the spelling words on the lines. Then have the students write the words inside the word search grid. Have them replace the empty spaces with random letters. Allow the students to trade word searches and solve them. A blank spelling word-search page has been provided for you on page 48.

Language, Writing, and Poetry Activities *(cont.)*

c. Spelling Concentration—Write spelling words on two sets of note cards. Place the cards face down. Have the students take turns drawing two cards each to try to get a match. The student with the most matches wins the game.

5. Play spelling word basketball. In teams, have the students practice spelling their words. When they spell a word correctly, allow them to shoot a basket. (You can use a trash can for a basket and a wad of paper for a ball.) Keep score and reward the spelling basketball winners.

6. Spelling word baseball is also a big hit. Divide your class into two teams. Set up imaginary bases in the classroom. Pitch a word to the student who is up to bat. If he or she spells the word correctly allow him or her to advance to first base. Then pitch the next student on that team a different word. Continue playing until three words are misspelled. Count those as three outs. Allow the opposing team to have their turn at bat. Enlist a scorekeeper to keep score and reward the winning team.

7. Guide Words Sports Chain—Have students make a vocabulary chain about a certain sport. At the top of the chain use the shape of a piece of equipment for that particular sport. On the links of the chain the students will write various vocabulary words that relate to the sport. Have the students write the word in the center of the chain link. On either side of the vocabulary word, the student will write the dictionary guide words which would help one to locate that word in a dictionary. Connect the links of the chain in alphabetical order. Hang the chains from the ceiling to create a festive mood in your classroom. Have a contest to see who can create the most links on their chain of words.

8. Sports Charades—Play sports charades. Act out or mime your favorite sports. Use the list of sports provided for the creation of the ABC book activity if you need a word bank for the game.

9. Career Awareness—Invite a doctor, nurse, sports therapist, coach, golf pro, aerobic instructor, or some other sports-related career person to visit your classroom. Remember to write thank you notes to the person who visits.

10. Have the students write concrete poems about sports. Show them an example of a sports shape on the overhead projector and write a description of the sport that the shape represents. For example, around the shape of a basketball, you might write this:

Shooting, running, jumping—this game is really pumping.

Dribbling, traveling, pivoting—this game is simply riveting.

11. Have the students write acrostics about their favorite sports. The following are examples:

Splash	**T**opspin	**S**ave
Wet	**E**lbow	**O**bstruction
In the pool	**N**et	**C**orner kick
Meet	**N**ylon	**C**hampionship
Medal	**I**ndoor	**E**xpel
Immerse	**S**erve	**R**estart
New swim suit		
Glide through the water		

Sports Search

Research your favorite sports. Use encyclopedias, books, computer software, and other research materials to answer the following questions:

Name of the sport you are researching: _____

_____

Where was this sport originally played?

_____

_____

What are the rules for this sport? _____

_____

_____

_____

_____

_____

_____

_____

_____

_____

_____

What special equipment is needed to play this sport? _____

_____

_____

_____

_____

Who are some famous people who participate in this sport?_____

_____

_____

_____

What are some interesting facts about this sport? _____

_____

_____

_____

Why is this your favorite sport?

_____

_____

The Sports Edition

Your are a sports reporter/editor. Use this page or design your own to report on two or more of your favorite recent sports events. (These may be real or made up.) When you are finished, trade with others in the class to read theirs. Gather all of the class reports to make a complete sports newspaper for display.

Sports in the News

Sports Story Web

Read a sports story about a famous sports figure. Use the following web to record information about the person. Use the information from your web to write a book report about the person. Publish your writing in a person-shaped book.

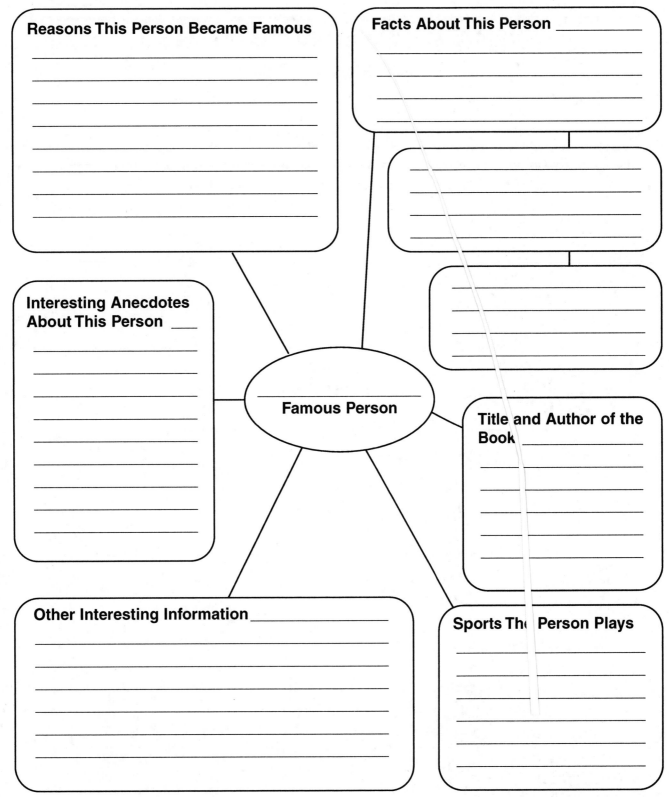

Reasons This Person Became Famous

Facts About This Person _____

Interesting Anecdotes About This Person ____

Famous Person _____

Title and Author of the Book _____

Other Interesting Information _____

Sports The Person Plays

Sports Are Where the Action Is

Verb Scavenger Hunt

Directions: Go on a scavenger hunt around your school. Look for actions that are occurring. Record the verbs that tell about the actions you find. Some examples might include *writing, sneezing, talking, running,* and *swinging*.

1. _____   11. _____

2. _____   12. _____

3. _____   13. _____

4. _____   14. _____

5. _____   15. _____

6. _____   16. _____

7. _____   17. _____

8. _____   18. _____

9. _____   19. _____

10. _____   20. _____

Sports Bingo

Write your spelling words randomly in the spaces below. When you hear the words called out, cover the space with a marker.

		FREE		

Spelling Word Search

Directions: Write your spelling words on the lines below. Then carefully rewrite them in the squares of the grid (only one letter per square). Arrange all the words going **up**, **down**, **across**, **diagonally**, or **backwards**. Fill in the empty squares that are left with random letters from the alphabet. When you have finished creating your word search, exchange it with a friend and solve each other's.

1. _____
2. _____
3. _____
4. _____
5. _____

6. _____
7. _____
8. _____
9. _____
10. _____

11. _____
12. _____
13. _____
14. _____
15. _____

16. _____
17. _____
18. _____
19. _____
20. _____

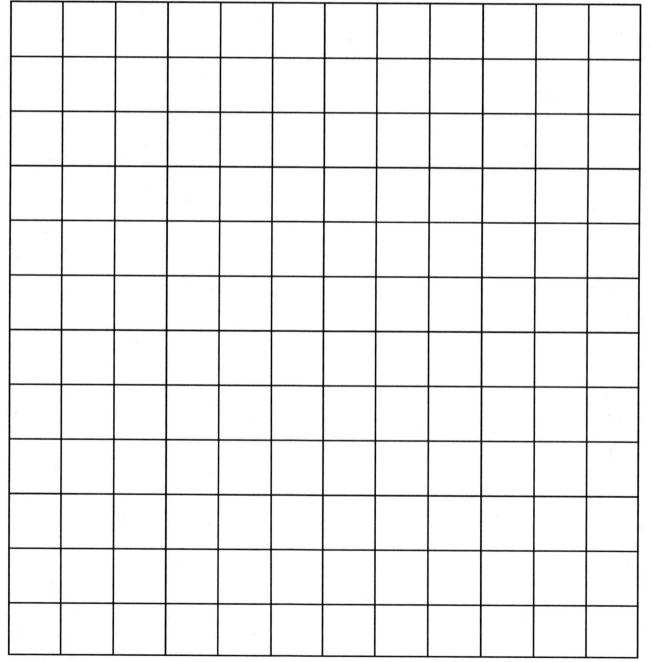

Sporty Postcards

Use the postcard patterns below to send postcards to friends about a favorite sport or sports. Remember to address the postcards correctly and write your information in paragraph form.

Sports Big Book

Materials

- 12" x 18" (30 cm x 46 cm) white construction paper for book pages and title page

- 12" x 18" (30 cm x 46 cm) colored construction paper for front and back cover of book

- assorted colors, sizes, and shapes of scrap construction paper

- writing paper for text

- crayons, colored pencils, and markers

- glue and scissors

Procedure

Each student will have a page in the big book to create. The teacher may want to have students sign up for different sports so the book will include a wider variety. After selecting the different sports to be included in the book, the students will use crayons, colored pencils, markers, or construction paper shapes to create a background for their pages in the book. Next, students will write paragraphs about the sports they signed up for. Make a title page for the front of your big book and have all your students sign the page. You may also want to include a comments page at the end of your big book for each student to write on. A sample title page and comments page have been included below. After the book is finished, number and laminate all the pages. After numbering the pages, you may want to add a table of contents to the beginning of your big book. Bind the book together, using a large book binder, notebook rings, or yarn laced through holes.

Crossword Sports Puzzle

Use the clues below to complete the crossword puzzle.

Across

3. The sport which uses a black-and-white checked ball
4. The object of this sport is to get a touchdown.
7. A scoring term used in tennis
8. The action most frequently performed on a soccer ball
10. The clothing worn by a swimmer

Down

1. A special term used to describe shirts worn in some sports events
2. The action of a bowling ball
5. A worldwide sports competition
6. Sports competitors
9. A good reason for people to participate in sports

1 _____
2 _____
3 _____
4 _____
5 _____

6 _____
7 _____
8 _____
9 _____
10 _____

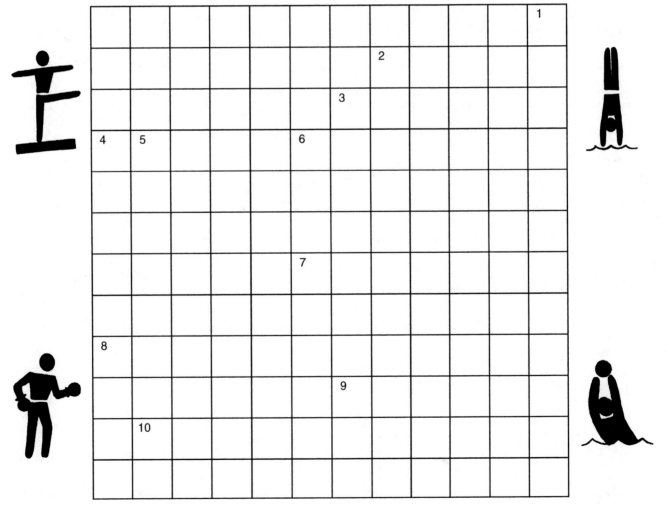

Challenge: See if you can add two or three more clues and sports words to this puzzle.

Compound Word Power

Strengthen your brain's muscles by giving them the following workout! Make compound sports words by combining the words in box A with the words in box B. Write the words in the proper sentences below.

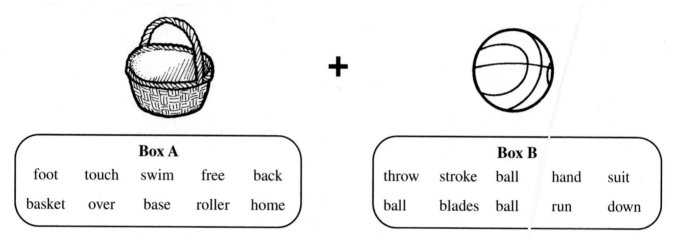

Box A

foot	touch	swim	free	back
basket	over	base	roller	home

Box B

throw	stroke	ball	hand	suit
ball	blades	ball	run	down

1. At the _____ game we watched the pitcher strike out three players in a row, for a no-hit inning.

2. This summer I am going to buy a new _____ to wear at the pool.

3. After the kickoff, our team ran the football 60 yards down the field and scored a _____.

4. *Dribbling, shooting, foul,* and *tip-off* are all terms used in the game of _____.

5. A _____ is something that occurs in baseball when a player hits the ball out of the park.

6. If you get fouled in the game of basketball, you may get to shoot a _____.

7. The _____ is a swimming stroke that is performed while lying on one's back in the water.

8. Baseball is different from softball because the pitcher throws the ball in an _____ motion rather than an underhand motion.

9. At a _____ game the field is marked in units of ten yards each.

10. _____ are shoes with wheels attached which are used to glide along on a smooth surface.

52

Invent a New Sport

Directions: Use your imagination to help create a new sport or game. You may want to combine two sports to create a totally new one, or you may want to create a sport that no one else has thought of. Use the questions below to help guide you through the process of creating your new sport.

1. What will the name of your sport or game be? _____

   Why? _____

2. How will this sport/game be played? _____

   _____

   _____

   _____

   _____

3. What type of equipment will be needed to play this sport/game?

   _____

   _____

4. How many people will play this sport/game at the same time? _____

5. What are the rules for this new sport/game?

   _____   _____

   _____   _____

   _____   _____

   _____   _____

6. Draw a picture of your new sport/game being played.

Practice teaching your new sport/game to a friend. Be prepared to teach the rest of the class how to play at a later date.

Favorite Sports Graph

Survey the students in your class about their favorite sports. Keep a tally of their responses. Use the data you collect to complete the sports graph below.

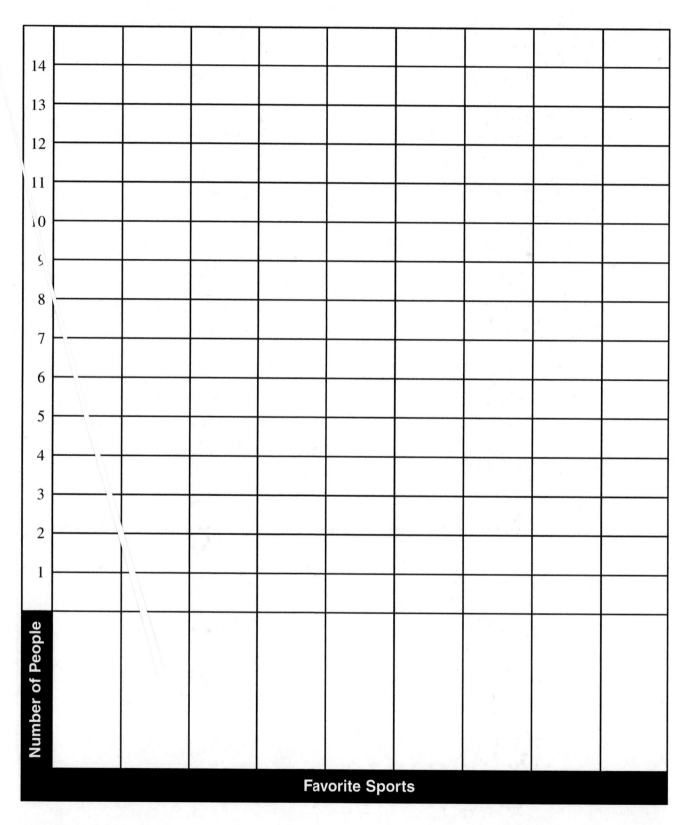

Favorite Sports

54   © *Teacher Created Materials, Inc.*

Sports Shapes Graph

Each person in your class should bring in a piece of equipment from a favorite sport. Place the equipment into groups according to their shapes. Complete the graph below to show how many pieces of each shape were brought in. Which shape is the most common sports shape (e.g., circle, oval, oblong, square, rectangle, other)? Which shape was the least common?

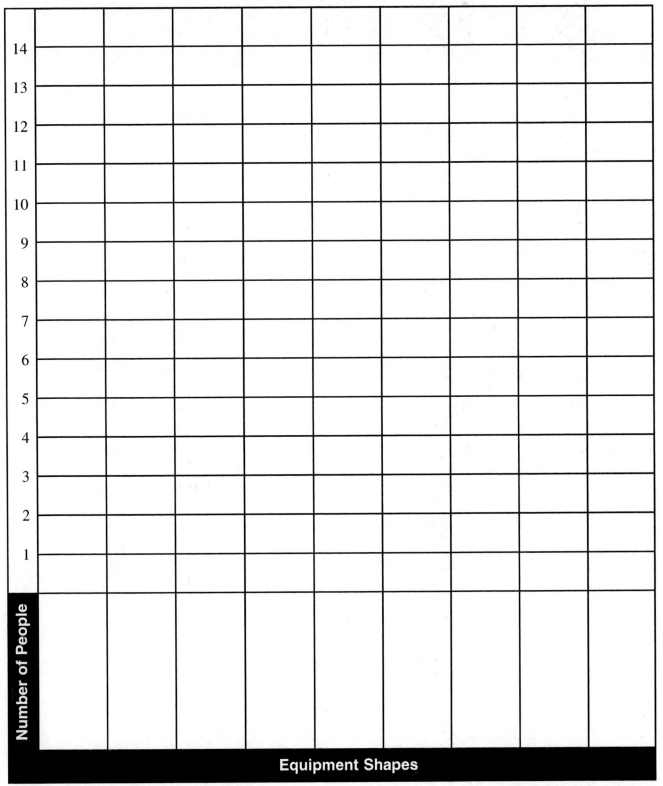

Sporting Goods Extravaganza

Visit a local sporting goods store with a member of your family. Record the brand name and the price of the sports equipment listed below. We will use the information you gather to create some problem-solving situations to challenge our class.

Item	Brand	Price
1. Basketball		
2. Baseball Glove		
3. Rollerblades		
4. Golf Balls		
5. Tennis Shoes		
6. Fishing Rod		
7. Football		
8. Soccer Ball		
9. Ice Skates		
10. Volleyball		
11. Bicycle		
12. Swimming Goggles		
13. Cleats		
14. Water Skis		
15. Tennis Racket		

Extra Credit:

List two additional pieces of sports equipment and their prices.

1. _____   _____   _____

2. _____   _____   _____

Sports Trivia

In your cooperative teams, create a list of 20 to 25 questions about sports. As a team find the answers to your questions. (You may already know some of the answers.) Use index cards to write your questions on one side and your answers on the other side. As a team create a game board and some game markers to use when playing the game.

You will need to create a list of directions for playing your game. You will also need to practice playing the game to make sure that your directions are complete and easily understood.

Use the space provided below to write down your ideas for the game. Then, meet with your cooperative team to begin creating your sports trivia game.

Questions	**Directions**
1. _____	_____
2. _____	_____
3. _____	_____
4. _____	_____
5. _____	_____
6. _____	_____
7. _____	_____
8. _____	_____
9. _____	_____
10. _____	_____
11. _____	
12. _____	
13. _____	
14. _____	
15. _____	
16. _____	
17. _____	
18. _____	
19. _____	
20. _____	

FINISH START

Game Board

Forward 3 spaces

BACK 2 spaces

Sports Around the World

Make a list of ten sports for which you would like to find the time and place of origin (along with one or two other interesting details). Use encyclopedias, CD-ROM programs, sports trivia books, and other reference materials to determine the region of the world in which each sport began and what year it began. An example has been done for you. Label your world map. Example: *Basketball*—Springfield, Massachusetts (U.S.A.), 1891. The first "basket" was actually a real peach basket.

1. _____

2. _____

3. _____

4. _____

5. _____

6. _____

7. _____

8. _____

9. _____

10. _____

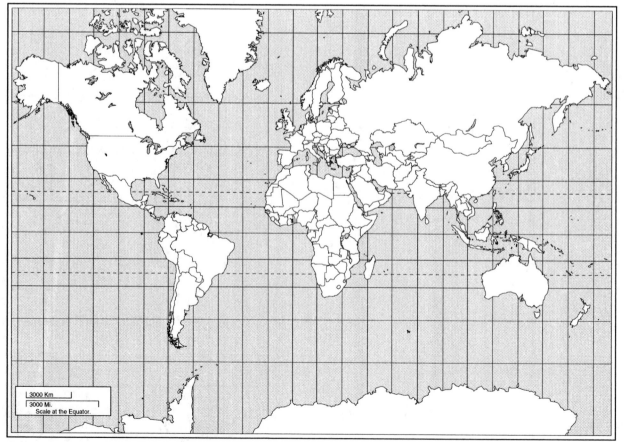

3000 Km
3000 Mi.
Scale at the Equator.

Sports Time Line

The first sports activities date so far back that historians are unable to place an exact date on their beginning. Most historians would agree that sports began the first time that a person used some physical energy to perform a task. Some of the first sports participated in were probably ones such as fishing or hunting, although these were actually necessities for survival rather than "games" or "sports." The first recorded Olympics dates back to 776 B.C. This event has been called the birth of organized sports events.

In some archaeological excavations, evidence has been found which suggests that the ancient Sumerians participated in the sport of wrestling about 5,000 years ago.

The Olympic Games were abolished in 394 A.D. and revived again in 1896. When they returned, many modern recording devices emerged, such as photographs, stopwatches, and newspaper reports. The Olympics games also brought about a more competitive aspect of playing sports. Originally, people played sports for pleasure or defense.

Around 1200 A.D., the French began playing a game similar to hockey by using sticks to knock a ball across the line. By the 1400s tennis was beginning to become popular also. Sporting events became increasingly popular in England during the 1500s. They lifted a ban they had placed on football (a modern version of soccer), and they began participating in other organized sporting activities, including golf and horse racing.

During the 1700s boxing increased in popularity as well as track and field events, rugby, and American-style football. Baseball did not officially emerge until the mid 1800s in the United States, and basketball was invented in 1891.

Sports events have continued to become popular throughout the world. The media have continued to increase coverage of sports events, and records have been kept on athletes in all areas of sports.

On the following pages are the names of famous sports figures and records they have set or amazing feats they have accomplished in the sports world. In your cooperative teams, create a time line like the one pictured below and glue the captions on the following pages in the correct order on the time line. You may also want to incorporate some of the historical information above into your team's time line. Add illustrations to go with the captions.

Sample Time Line

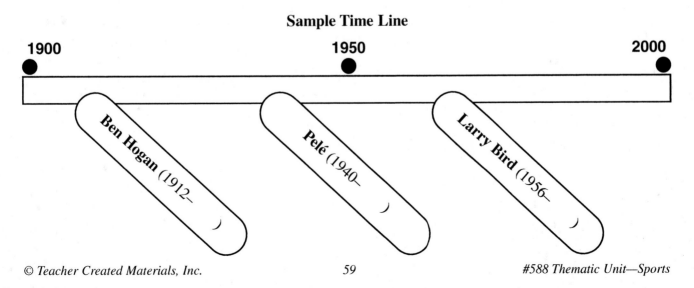

Sports Time Line (cont.)

Joe Louis (1914–1981)—He became the heavyweight boxing champion in 1937. He defended his title 25 times.

Willie Mays (1931–   )—He was the first player in professional baseball to hit 600 homeruns during a career. He began playing baseball with the New York Giants where he won the Rookie-of-the-Year award. He retired from baseball after hitting 660 homeruns and 3,283 total hits.

Olga Korbut (1955–   )—She is a Soviet gymnast who won three gold medals for her routines in the 1972 Olympic games. She is extremely flexible on the balance beam. She helped to stimulate worldwide interest in the field of gymnastics because of her performance in the 1976 Olympic games.

Chris Evert (1954–   )—She was ranked as the world's leading woman tennis player in 1974–1978 and again in 1980–1981. She has won titles at Wimbledon in 1974, 1976, and 1981. She retired in 1989 with 157 professional singles titles. This was an all-time record in the field of tennis.

Larry Bird (1956–   )—He is an American basketball player who is thought of as one of the best forwards and all-around players in the history of basketball. He was named the NBA's most valuable player in 1984, 1985, and 1986.

Ty Cobb (1886–1961)—He played baseball for the Detroit Tigers and the Philadelphia Athletics. He was outstanding in almost every aspect of the game of baseball. He set records for his batting average, his runs scored, and the number of batting titles he won.

Ben Hogan (1912–   )—He was a professional golfer during the 1940s and 1950s. He was professional golf's leading money winner during five seasons. He formed the Ben Hogan Company, a golfing equipment firm, at the end of his career and has been very successful.

Jesse Owens (1913–1980)—He was an American track star who competed in the 1936 Olympic games. He won four gold medals. He placed first in the 100 meter sprint, the 200 meter sprint, and the broad jump. He was also a part of the winning United States 400 meter relay team.

Joe Namath (1943–   )—He was a quarterback for the University of Alabama. He led this team to three bowl games and a national championship. He became the highest paid athlete of the time when he signed a $427,000 contract in 1965 with the New York Jets. His greatest success on record was when he led the Jets to the 1969 Super Bowl victory.

60

Sports Time Line *(cont.)*

Pelé (1940–   )—He was a Brazilian soccer player who became one of the world's wealthiest and most famous athletes. He led his team in Brazil to three World Cup championships in 1958, 1962, and 1970. He is credited with advancing the popularity of soccer in the United States. In 1975 he was recruited to play for the New York Cosmos and was given a contract for 4 million dollars.

Babe Ruth (1948–1985)—He is considered one of the most famous baseball players of all time. He began his career as a pitcher for the Boston Red Sox. He was then recruited by the New York Yankees, where he became an outfielder. He is credited with leading the New York Yankees to four world championships in baseball.

Mario Andretti (1940–   )—He is a famous race car driver. He has competed successfully in sprint car racing, midget racing, stock car racing, and Indianapolis-style racing. He held a closed-circuit speed record until 1974.

Peggy Fleming (1948–   )—She was an Olympic figure skater in the 1968 Olympics. She won a gold medal.

Joan Benoit (1957–   )—She won a gold medal in the first Olympic woman's marathon in the 1984 Olympic games. She was also the first woman to finish the Boston Marathon in 1979.

Greg Louganis (1960–   )—He was only 16 years old when he won a gold medal for diving in the 1976 Olympic games. He has since won four Olympic gold medals, six Pan American games gold medals, five world championships, and 47 United States titles in diving.

Nancy Lopez (1957--   )—She is a professional golf star. In 1978 alone, she won nine tournaments.

Pete Rose (1941–   )—He holds many major league baseball records. He is most famous for his 4,256 hits during his career.

Henry Aaron (1934–   )—He is famous for hitting the most home runs in the history of baseball. He was an outfielder for the Atlanta Braves. He was elected to the Baseball Hall of Fame in 1982.

Rocky Marciano (1923–1969)—He is the only professional heavyweight champion in boxing who retired undefeated. He won the heavyweight crown in 1952.

Jackie Robinson (1919–1972)—He was the first black American baseball player to play in the major leagues. He began playing in 1947 for the Brooklyn Dodgers. He helped his team win the pennant and won the Most Valuable Player of the Year award in 1949.

Sports Time Line *(cont.)*

Jim Brown (1936–   )—He was a leading rusher for a period of time in professional football. He played for the Philadelphia Eagles and the Cleveland Browns. He retired from football in 1965 to begin an acting career.

Bjorn Borg (1956–   )—He is a Swedish tennis player who began playing professionally at the age of 14. In 1976 he won the first of five Wimbledon singles titles.

Jack Nicklaus (1940–   )—He is an American golfer who has won each of the four Grand Slam golfing events. He won the Masters, the U.S. Open, the PGA Open, and the British Open. He designs golf courses also.

Bob Cousy (1928–   )—He was a basketball star known for his outstanding ball handling abilities. He earned the honor of Most Valuable Player in 1957.

Mary Decker (1958–   )—She is an American track star. She held many track record for women in the 1970s and 1980s.

Philip Anthony Esposito (1942–   )—He was a famous center in hockey. He was the first hockey player to score more than 100 points. He was voted Hockey's Most Valuable Player twice.

Michael Jordan (1963–   )—He led the National Basketball Association in scoring for five consecutive years. He led the Chicago Bulls to the NBA championship in 1991.

Dorothy Hamill (1956–   )—She was an Olympic figure skater. She won a gold medal in the 1976 winter Olympics in Innsbruck.

Joe Montana (1956–   )—He was a football quarterback during the 1980s. He is known for his high percentage of pass completions. He holds some regular-season awards as well as some Super Bowl awards.

Sonja Henie (1912–1969)—Born in Norway, she won her first world figure skating title at the age of 13. A holder of six European titles and 10 world titles, she captured Olympic gold medals in 1928, 1932, and 1936 to dominate the world of figure skating then.

Babe Didrikson Zaharias (1914–1969)—Born in Texas, she entered the 1932 Olympics, winning gold medals in the javelin and hurdles and a silver medal in the high jump. Between 1940 and 1950 she won 82 amateur and professional golf tournaments and was named the Outstanding Female Athlete of the first half century by the Associated Press.

62

Why Exercise?

Use the columns below to brainstorm various types of exercises, reasons to exercise, and good exercise habits. Record your ideas on the chart.

Types of Exercise	Reasons to Exercise	Good Exercise Habits

Exercise Record

Exercise Record for _____

Use this chart to keep a record of your daily exercise habits. Record your exercise and sports activities and the amount of time you participated in each activity. Use the chart to determine if you are getting enough exercise each week. If you are not, try to increase the number of days or the length of time that you exercise.

Date	Type of Exercise/Sports	Amount of Time

Hearts in Motion

Each individual has a rate at which his or her heart beats. The beating of your heart is called your pulse. When you are resting, your heart rate (pulse) will be different from what it is when you are exercising. You can check your pulse by placing your fingers in certain places on your body. Many people are able to feel the pulse on the insides of their wrists. This is accomplished by placing your first two fingers on top of the veins in your wrist. Your thumb can be used to support the back side of your hand. If you are unable to feel a pulse from this vein, you may want to try the artery in your neck. To find this artery, gently place the same first two fingers in the middle of your neck. Then move them to either side of your neck about one inch. You should feel a pulse in this position. It is important that you not press too tightly in this area.

Once you are able to feel your pulse, you should be able to find out what your resting heart rate is and what your heart rate right after exercise is. Have a partner assist you by keeping time for you. You will want to count the number of pulse beats that you feel during a one-minute period of time.

First, you should take your pulse while sitting at your desk. Record your resting heart rate below.

Next, jog in place for a few minutes. Now take your pulse again. Below, record your heart rate after exercising.

Resting Heart Rate: _____

After-Exercise Heart Rate: _____

Answer the following questions:

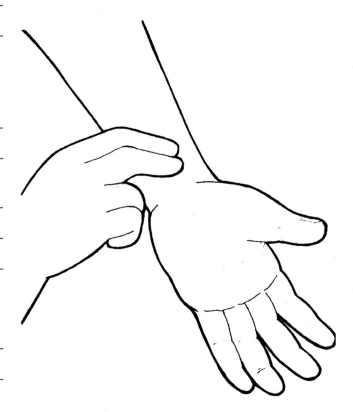

- When did your heart beat the fastest?

  _____

  _____

- What was the difference between the two heart rates?_____

  _____

  _____

- Does exercise increase or decrease the rate at which your heart beats?

  _____

  _____

- Why do you think it is important to increase the rate of your heart? _____

  _____

  _____

Hearts-in-Motion Diagram

Your heart is a very complex organ in your body. It pumps blood to all the regions in your body. It uses arteries and veins as tunnels to transport the blood to the rest of your body. Below is a diagram of the heart. Use it to label the parts of the heart and to learn how the blood travels.

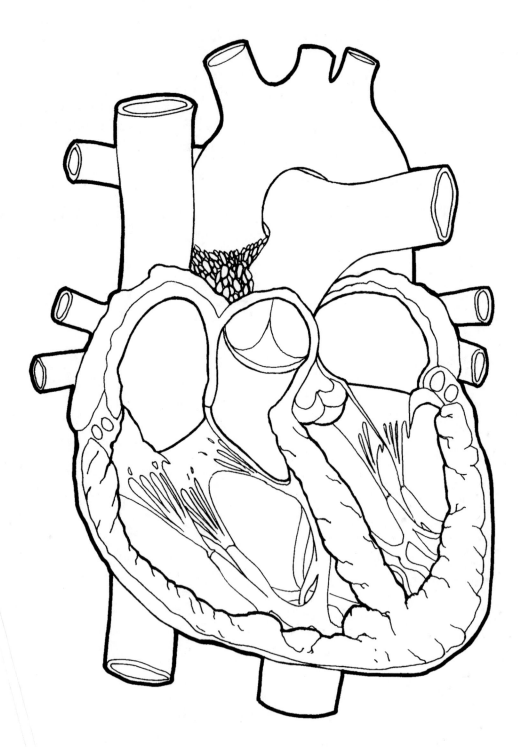

Flex Those Muscles!

Your muscles play an important role in your body, especially if you participate in sports. Your muscles are the organs that help you move your body. There are different kinds of muscles in your body that allow you to move in different ways. Some muscles you cannot control. These muscles are called *involuntary* muscles. Some of these involuntary muscles help you to breathe, blink your eyes, and pump your heart. Muscles that you are able to control are called *voluntary* muscles. You use these muscles to help you lift objects, turn your head from left to right, walk, and eat.

Your muscles work by *contracting*. Contracting a muscle makes the muscle become shorter and thicker. You can observe a contracting muscle by holding your arm out straight to your side and slowly lifting and bending it at your elbow. The muscle in your upper arm will become shorter and thicker. You can probably feel the difference in the thickness.

Your bones and muscles work together inside your body. Your bones are connected to your muscles by special tissues called *tendons*. A tendon is what causes the bones to move when your muscle contracts.

Use the information above to help you answer the questions below:

1. What is an involuntary muscle?_____

   _____

   _____

2. What types of movements are caused by voluntary muscles? _____

   _____

   _____

3. When a muscle becomes shorter and thicker, it _____.

4. What is the main purpose of your muscles? _____

   _____

   _____

5. What are the two kinds of muscles? _____

   _____

6. When a muscle contracts, the _____ causes the bone to move.

7. What type of muscle do you use when you are breathing or sitting in a chair listening to music?

   _____

8. Bones and muscles are connected together by _____.

Challenge: What types of muscles did you use to complete this activity?

_____

_____

_____

Sports Medicine

Directions: Use the information in the paragraphs below to answer the questions at the bottom of the page.

 The field of sports medicine is one that deals with the treatment and prevention of injuries that occur while playing sports. It also includes the scientific research charged with determining the causes and possible treatments of various sports injuries.

Athletes must perform different movements, depending on the type of sports they participate in. The physicians who treat sports injuries have identified six basic motions in sports. They include the stance, walking, running, jumping, kicking, and throwing. Various sports contain one, a combination, or all of these motions.

There are some specific types of sports injuries that are treated most often by doctors. The most common injuries are tennis elbow, shoulder injuries, back injuries, leg and ankle injuries, and knee injuries. Some athletes are treated for substance use, and the reasons for this abuse along with its treatment are part of sports medicine as well.

• What is sports medicine? _____

_____

_____

• What types of research do physicians in the field of sports medicine conduct? _____

_____

Why? _____

_____

_____

• What are the six basic motions that athletes use in sports? _____

_____

_____

• What are some reasons you think an athlete might need treatment for substance use and abuse?

_____

_____

• Have you ever had a sports injury? If so, describe what happened to you and tell briefly how you were treated for your injury. _____

_____

_____

Sports Medicine Bones Diagram

The human skeletal system is made up of 206 bones. The bones are held together by connective tissues, ligaments, and tendons. Your skeleton has three main jobs:

- **It is supposed to protect your important organs.**

- **It should help your body with movement.**

- **It should provide your body with support.**

The skeletal system is also important because the bones produce blood cells.

Use the diagram below to help you learn the names of the bones in your body.

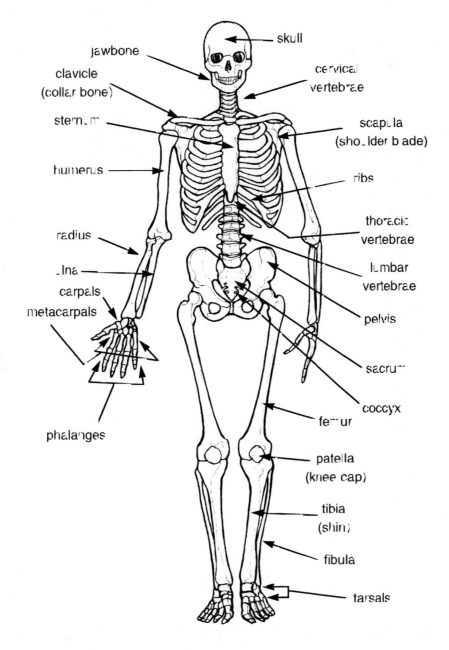

Design a Sports Award

Use the certificate pattern below to design a sports award for someone in your class. Keep in mind that sports awards can be given for a number of different reasons. Be sure to write on the award the specific reason you are giving it to that person. Cut the award out and mount it on a piece of colored construction paper. Place the award in a safe place until the Sports Convention Day. Then honor your friend by giving him or her the award at the convention.

Favorite Sport Diorama

A diorama is a scene that is recreated inside a box. In this activity, you will be creating a diorama of your favorite sport. You may want your scene to be about something that actually happened to you or someone else, or you may want to create a totally new scene.

Materials

- empty boxes of assorted sizes
- glue and scissors
- construction paper of assorted sizes, colors, and shapes
- markers, crayons, colored pencils
- assorted craft materials

Procedures

Make a diorama of your favorite sport. Use the materials above to create a scene replicating your favorite sport being played. You will want to give some of your characters a three-dimensional appearance by standing them up in or on your diorama. You may want to draw a picture on paper before beginning the diorama to help you brainstorm an idea for your scene. Be sure to give your scene a title. When you are finished, display your diorama in your classroom. Some sample dioramas have been drawn below to help you get started. Remember: be original and be creative!

Sports Collage

There are many exciting words and actions which are used in sports. Search through magazines and newspapers to find as many of the words and actions as you can. Then create a collage to display the excitement of sports.

Materials

- old newspaper
- old magazines
- 12" x 18" (30 cm x 46 cm) colored construction paper

- glue
- scissors
- crayons, markers, colored pencils

Procedures

Create a collage of exercise/sports words and pictures. Use the magazines and newspapers to cut out sports pictures and words. (Remember that action words are great sports words!) Arrange the pictures and words that you find in an attractive, eye-catching manner on your construction paper. Include a title for your collage in the middle of your construction paper. You may want to represent the title of your collage by cutting out the letters for the title from newspaper or magazine headlines. Include small illustrations of the words you find by using your colored pencils, crayons, or markers. Begin gluing the words and pictures down after you are pleased with the layout of your design. Once your collage is dry, display it in your classroom.

Sports Convention

Plan a Sports Convention to end your sports study.

❏ Have students dress up as their favorite sports personalities. When they arrive at school on the day of the sports convention, take their pictures to display at a later date. Allow them to have an autograph session where they sign the Famous People in Sports autograph page on page 74.

❏ Have students give oral presentations about their favorite persons in sports. Use the Sports Biography activity (page 20) as a guide for the oral presentations.

❏ Use the Invent a New Sport activity on page 53 and allow your students the opportunity to teach their new sport to the class. Have plenty of sports equipment on hand so that you are prepared for the events to take place.

❏ Have a sharing session where you allow your students to share their favorite parts of the sports unit. You might want to make a chart of what your students learned throughout the unit and display it on your wall.

❏ Have students work together in teams to create a display of a favorite sport. Have them include on their display a brief history of the sport, pictures of famous athletes who participate in that sport, the rules of how to play that sport, trivia questions about that sport, books about that sport, and other additional information they find about that sport. Have them set their display up in an area of the classroom to be used as a center by the other students. A sample of what one of these displays might look like appears on page 75. Give your students a copy of this page to help guide them in making their own sports displays.

❏ Reread some of your favorite stories from the sports unit.

❏ Allow your students to bring in their own sports awards, trophies, and certificates to share with the class. Provide an area in your classroom to place these awards.

❏ Present classroom awards for the sports unit. Use the awards on pages 77 and 78 and use the student-created awards from page 70. Your students will love receiving awards for their hard work during this unit.

❏ Challenge another class to a kickball game (or other sport) outside. Review the rules and discuss good sportsmanship before playing. Invite parents to watch the activities. You may want to enlist some parent volunteers to provide snacks for your students after the game.

❏ Organize a Sportsmanship Hall of Fame. Research and record exceptional acts of sportsmanship (as opposed to generally accepted sports achievements) by amateur or professional athletes. Examples are not unusual in the sport of golf, where players frequently call penalties on themselves, sometimes even disqualifying themselves from a tournament for a rule infraction. *Be sure to consider students sportsmen at your own school.* Prepare a poster, bulletin board, display, or big book describing the details, circumstances, and actions that merit your election of these persons to your Sportsmanship Hall of Fame.

Famous People in Sports
Autograph Page

74

Sports Display

In your cooperative team create a display about your favorite sport. Decide as a team which sport you will create your display about. Then, use the information you have learned during our sports study to create a display board about that sport. Let one section include a brief history of your sport, telling where it originated and a little background information on the sport. Let another section include the rules for your sport. The third section should be about some famous people who participate in this sport. You might also want to include some trivia questions about this sport. Next, provide some colorful illustrations of your sport. Arrange all of your information attractively on a display board. Neatness and creativity are encouraged. Below is a sample of what your board might look like when you finish.

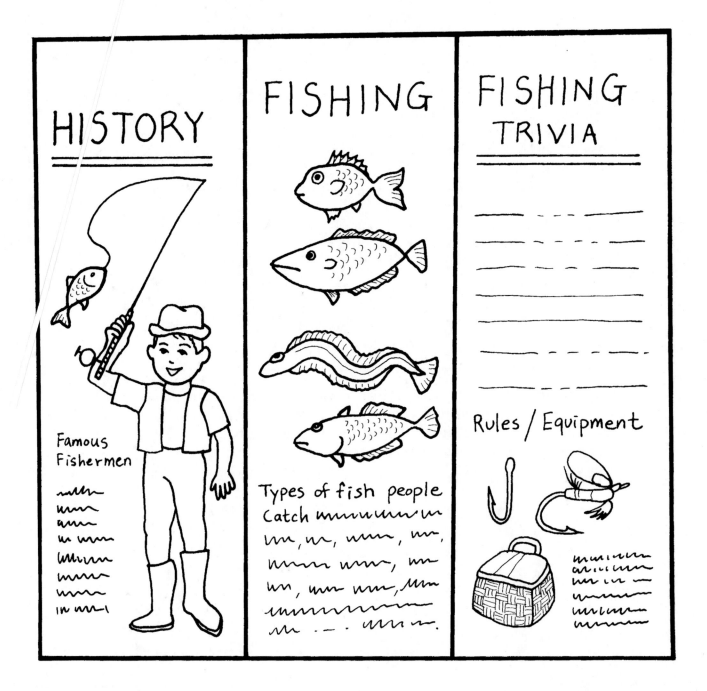

Bulletin Board Ideas

1. **Slam Dunk Spellers**—Use a picture of a basketball player slam dunking a basketball into a net. Display students' spelling papers on the bulletin board.

2. **Sports Views in the News**—Create a current events bulletin board about sports. Entitle the bulletin board "Sports Views in the News." Have the students bring in current events articles about sports events and display the articles on the board. You can expand this activity by having the students write summaries of their articles or by having them share what their articles are about.

3. **Sports Around the World**—Make a large drawing or replica of the world to put in the center of the bulletin board. Use pictures of different sports to place around the world. Have your students research the origins of the sports on the board and connect the sports picture to the place in the world that it originated. Students might use yarn and push pins to connect the pictures to the world.

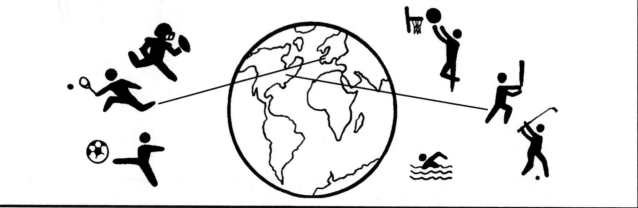

Sports Award

This award is given in
honor of_____
for _____

_____

_____

Today's Date:_____

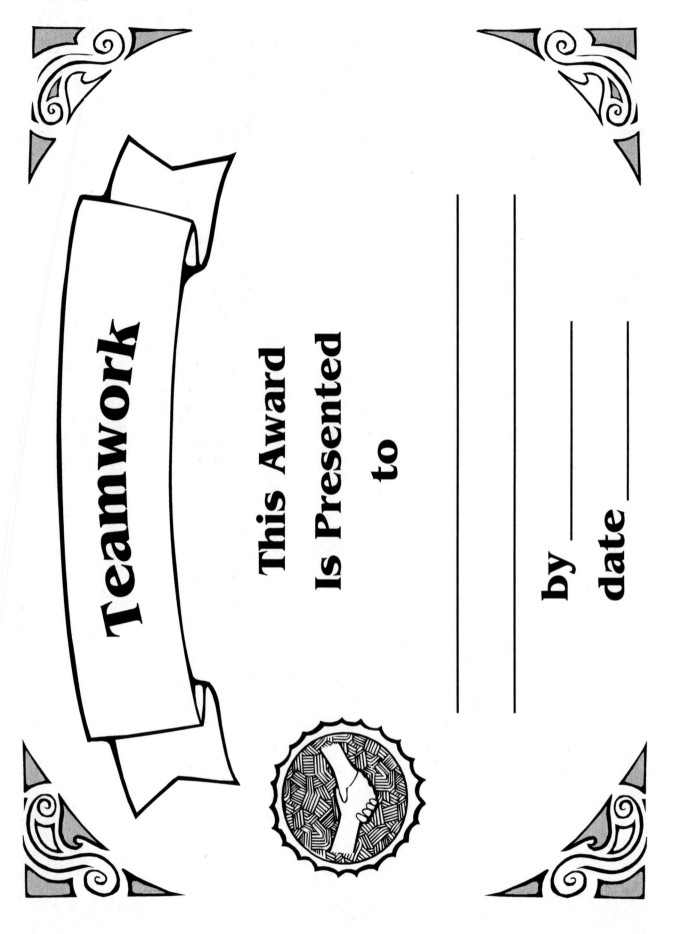

Teamwork

This Award Is Presented to

by _____

date _____

78

Bibliography

Fiction

Bach, Alice. *The Meat in the Sandwich*. Harper & Row, 1975.

Cole, Joanna. *The Magic School Bus® Lost in the Human Body*. Scholastic, 1989.

Dragonwagon, Crescent. *Annie Flies the Birthday Bike*. Macmillan, 1993.

Giff, Patricia Reilly. *Ronald Morgan Goes to Bat*. Penguin Books, 1988.

Maestro, Betsy and Giulo. *Bike Trip*. Harper Collins, 1992.

Marzollo, Jean. *Soccer Sam*. Random House, 1987.

Parrish, Peggy. *Amelia Bedelia Goes Camping*. Greenwillow, 1985.

Shannon, David. *How George Radbourn Saved Baseball*. Blue Sky/Scholastic, 1994.

Sobol, Donald J. *Encyclopedia Brown's Book of Wacky Sports*. Morrow, 1984.

Thayer, Ernest Lawrence. *Casey at the Bat*. G.P. Putnam's Sons, 1988.

Poetry

Adoff, Arnold. *Sports Pages*. J.B. Lippincott, 1986.

Knudson, R.R. and Swenson, May. *American Sports Poems*. Orchard Books, 1988.

Nonfiction

Arnold, Caroline. *The Olympic Summer Games*. Franklin Watts, 1991.

Arthur, Lee. *Sports Math: How It Works*. Lothrop, Lee & Shepard, 1975.

Fradin, Dennis. *Olympics*. Regensteiner, 1983.

Golenbock, Peter and Paul Bacon. *Teammates*. Golenbock Comm., Inc., 1990.

Hammond, Tim. *Sports*. Knopf, 1988.

Jennings, Jay. *Teamwork: United in Victory*. Silver Burdett Press, 1990.

Litsky, Frank. *The Winter Olympics*. Franklin Watts, 1979.

May, Julian, *The Winter Olympics*. Creative Education Children's Press, 1976.

Nash, Bruce & Zullo, Allan. *The Greatest Sports Stories Never Told*. Little Simon, 1993.

O'Connor, Jim. *Comeback*. Random House, 1992.

Pretner, Lee. *Pro Sports Trivia*. Watts, 1975.

Schneider, Tom. *Everybody's a Winner: A Kid's Guide to New Sports*. Little Brown, 1976.

Jokes and Riddles

Bernstein, Joanne E. *Sporty Riddles*. A. Whitman, 1989.

Schultz, Sam. *101 Sports Jokes*. Lerner, 1982.

Music

1. "Take Me Out to the Ballgame" (lyrics by Jack Northwork, music by Albert Von Tilzer.)

Videos

1. *Pistol Pete* (Rated G)—This movie is about a young boy's pursuit of his dream to play basketball.

2. *Mighty Ducks* (Rated PG)—You will want to get parental permission to show this video. This movie is a wonderful story about the value of working together as a team.

3. *Time Out for Hilarious Sports Bloopers*. Front Row Video, Inc.

4. *Cool Runnings* (Rated PG)—You will want to get parental permission to show this video. This is an inspiring movie about the first Jamaican Olympic bobsled team. It has a great message for kids about finishing the race!

Answer Key

Football Frolics (page 23)

1. Atlanta 22, San Francisco 18
2. Dallas 42, Washington 42, tie game
3. Answers will vary.
4. Denver 35, Pittsburgh 20
5. Cleveland lost

Bonus: Answers will vary.

Swimming with the Alphabet (page 31)

1. *backstroke*
2. *breaststroke*
3. *breathing*
4. *butterfly*
5. *cannonball*
6. *dive*
7. *diving board*
8. *dog paddle*
9. *flips*
10. *float*
11. *free-style*
12. *glide*
13. *kick*
14. *lake*
15. *lanes*
16. *lifeguard*
17. *medley*
18. *ocean*
19. *plunge*
20. *pool*
21. *splash*
22. *springboards*
23. *swimsuit*
24. *takeoff*
25. *twists*

Crossword Sports Puzzle (page 51)

Across

3. *soccer*
4. *football*
7. *love*
8. *kick*
10. *swimsuit*

Down

1. *jersey*
2. *roll*
5. *Olympics*
6. *athletes*
9. *fun*

Compound Word Power (page 52)

1. *baseball*
2. *swimsuit*
3. *touchdown*
4. *basketball*
5. *homerun*
6. *freethrow*
7. *backstroke*
8. *overhand*
9. *football*
10. *rollerblades*